Orleton in Pictures

by

Ann and Alf Jenkins

Published by
Ann & Alf Jenkins,
Bower House, Orleton,
Nr. Ludlow, Shropshire.
SY8 4HR

Published 1996

© 1996, A. E. Jenkins

ISBN 0 95 09 274 14

Printed in England by Orphans Press Ltd., Hereford Road, Leominster, Herefordshire.

Contents

Acknowledgements

We would like to thank all the kind folk who have loaned us photographs for the collection, given us information and spent many hours identifying individuals.

The following deserve a special mention:-

Mr. David Williams; Mrs. Betty Cadwallader; Mrs. I. Wall; Mr. R. Dann; Mrs. A. Butcher; Mrs. R. Patrick; Mrs. L. Collins; Mrs. Mabel Wood; Mr. L. Stokes; Miss E. Radnor; Miss B. Wickstead; Mrs. K. Collings and the late Mr. Jim Collings; Mrs. J. Edwards; Mrs. Andrea Walters; Mr. Vic Ingram; Mrs. H. Roberts; Mrs. M. Godding; Pat of Paignton; Mrs. W. Faulkner; Mrs. Hetty Bloom; Mr. and Mrs. C. Roberts; Mr. and Mrs. C. Marsden; Mr. Graham Hodgetts; Mrs. Ena Sparey; Mr. Phil Postons and family; Mr. and Mrs. M. Sparey; Mr. and Mrs. Alf Sparey; Mr. Reg Grosvenor; Mrs. Betty Wood; Mrs. Beattie Woodfield; Miss Greta Bentley; Mrs. Ivy Bowen; Mr. Graham Nottingham; Mr. and Mrs. Bill Williams; Mr. Jim Ingram; Mr. and Mrs. J. Worthing; Mr. G. Crofts; Mrs. M. Worthing; Mrs. Pat Morgan; Mr. R. Fortey; Mrs. J. Rutter; Dr. P. Cross; Mrs. E. Powles; Mrs. Underwood; Mrs. Sue Moss; Mr. Viv Proctor; Mr. and Mrs. B. Harris.

Extracts from Mr. G. Platt's articles. By kind permission of his wife Madge.

The Late Mr. Ernest Selby for photography.

Mr. Peter Bartlett for his expertise, advice and copying old photographs.

Leominster News, Hereford Evening News, Ludlow Advertiser and Shropshire Star.

Airpic Aerial Photography for permission to use the photograph of Orleton for the cover.

Introduction

In 1986 Rector Peter Walter came to Orleton as Priest in Charge. By Spring of 1987 with the help of the P.C.C. he had made a synopsis of urgent restoration work needed in St. George's Church. Surveys informed us that the astronomical sum of £22,000 was required.

An appeal was launched and the Committee decided to hold a Victorian week-end during the August Bank Holiday. Mr. Geoff Crofts and I were responsible for organising an historical tour of the village. We mapped out a route to include the church, old school and numerous old properties in Church Lane, King's Road and Millbrook.

Geoff had a good collection of photographs of many of the black and white and stone properties; we appealed in the press for others. As a result we were able to display photographs and historical information outside each property. Duplicate copies were available for sale at the Village Hall Craft Fair.

So many questions were asked and requests for photographs made that we decided to formulate an "Orleton in Pictures" book. This collection will enable present and future residents to appreciate changes which have taken place here especially since the 1960s and hopefully will recall nostalgic memories to many.

It is always a problem to know when to call a halt to research and collections of photographs, but, I will take the advice of my past history master Frank Reeves who said to me when I was collating "Titterstone Clees" - "Stop now. There will always be more research to do and photographs which will appear afterwards."

Alf Jenkins.

Orleton in the Ice Age
by kind permission of Dr. P. Cross, M.Sc., Ph.D.

During the last glaciation of Britain a glacier moving from the Welsh Uplands down the Wye Valley spread out into Herefordshire. In the north of the county the ice front reached Orleton where it was stationary for a considerable time. The ice blocked the southward flow of a pre-glacial river which occupied the valley between Ludlow and Leominster and dammed up a glacial lake, Lake Woofferton. This Lake extended northwards from Orleton covering the Woofferton area and reaching Stanton Lacy to the north of Ludlow. It also extended eastwards down the present Teme Valley to beyond Tenbury where it overflowed. Downcutting by the overflow in the soft Downtonian rocks lowered the level of the lake and eventually resulted in it being drained and a new course being formed for the present day Teme, which now flows eastwards to join the Severn below Worcester. The old valley between Orleton and Leominster (followed by the railway) is now riverless.

The ridge on which Orleton stands is made up of clay, silt, sand, gravel and boulders deposited as the ice melted. It is in fact a moraine. A few years ago deep excavations for the sewage pumping station at Comberton revealed that just beyond the ice front there had been a number of small pools. These had been filled in by the meltwater from the glacier and had fostered plant life and insect life before being filled in and covered over by outwash gravel. In one of these old pools, remains of plants were found together with fossil beetles. These remains have given up a clear indication of the climatic conditions which existed at Orleton at the end of the last glaciation. They indicate an open treeless landscape with patchy vegetation cover. Most of the species of beetles which lived in the Comberton Pool (below the pumping station) are no longer found in the British Isles. Many are today restricted to Tundra regions in Scandinavia and Siberia. There is no doubt that the climate at the time was extremely cold. Radio carbon dating of moss remains found in the pool at Comberton gave a date of 12,000 B.P. (See Glacial Lake Map).

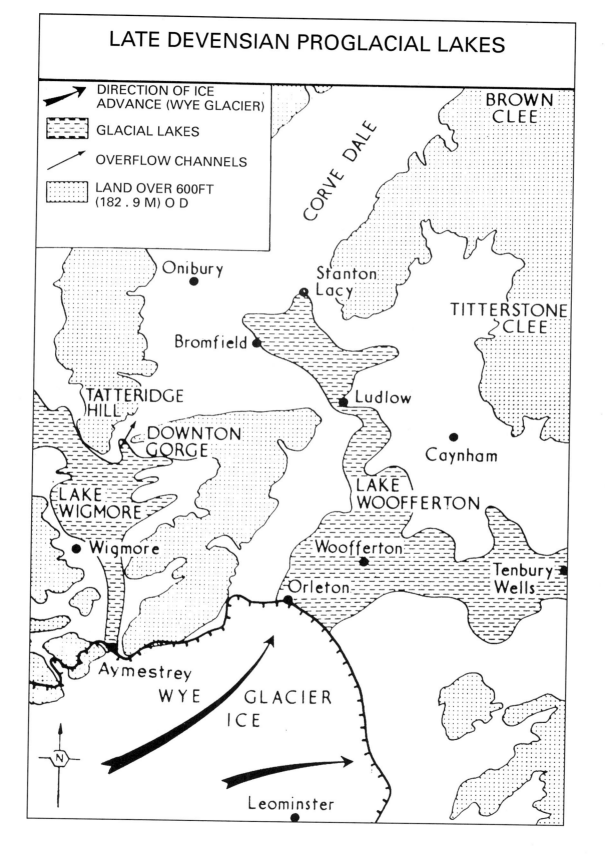

LATE DEVENSIAN PROGLACIAL LAKES

DIRECTION OF ICE
ADVANCE (WYE GLACIER)

GLACIAL LAKES

OVERFLOW CHANNELS

LAND OVER 600FT
(182.9 M) O D

BROWN
CLEE

CORVE DALE

Onibury

Stanton
Lacy

TITTERSTONE
CLEE

Bromfield

TATTERIDGE
HILL

Ludlow

DOWNTON
GORGE

Caynham

LAKE
WIGMORE

LAKE
WOOFFERTON

Wigmore

Woofferton

Orleton

Tenbury
Wells

Aymestrey

WYE   GLACIER
ICE

N

Leominster

5

Orleton

In Domesday Book Orleton is spelt ALRETVNE (the enclosure of the Alders) and it is interesting to note that we still have alder trees along the brookside in the 1990s. It was a timber traditionally used for making clogs. I wonder if ancient Orletonians wore them?

The Manor of Orleton was given by William the Conqueror to Ralph de Mortimer. It records Orleton as being in the Wolphy Hundred and Queen Edith held it.

"There are 4 hides of land which pay tax.

In Lordship there are 4 plough teams with 11 villagers, 15 smallholders, a reeve (magistrate) a rider; between them 7 ploughs, 6 slaves, 5 ploughmen and 1 smith.

The value before Domesday was £7. When the Manor was given to Ralph de Mortimer the Manor contained:-

4 hides taxable on the demesne lands, XI villiens, XV cottagers, a steward and a radman (a cultivator) with V1 plough teams. There were 6 serfs, five cow-herds and a blacksmith and the rental was reduced to 100 shillings.

It may help to mention that a hide was a measure of land calculated by the amount which could be ploughed by one man and one ox in one year. That could range from 160 acres down to 20 or so depending on the quality of land. I've no doubt therefore that in Orleton "the 4 hides which pay tax" exceeded 600 acres. Demesne lands meant that retained by in this case Ralph de Mortimer for his use; and the villiens etc who lived on it would be obligated to give free service. The villiens were a little higher in the pecking order than serfs but they had very few privileges. Note the 'steward' too. He was the person left in charge in the absence of Ralph de Mortimer. William the Conqueror put a tax valuation on all his new possessions and it would be interesting to know why Orleton Manor commanded less after Domesday.

To make a few comparisons it was known that Stoke-St-Milborough was valued at £13 and Burwarton (towards Bridgnorth) was 2/-. We can deduce from these figures therefore that Orleton was still well placed in the valuation stakes.

This is not a history of Orleton but the authors do hope that it will whet appetites and encourage others to fill in the gaps and delve deeper.

Orleton is so near the Welsh Marches, Wigmore, Mortimer's Cross, Ludlow and Offa's Dyke that its life must have continued to be very unsettled throughout the Middle Ages. There can be no doubt that the villiens and cottagers would have had no alternative when ordered by their Lord but to take up arms and fight for whatever cause he happened to support at the time.

And so Orleton has been a community at the centre of historical events and steeped in farming for a very long time.

Moving forward to the Victorian era Mr. Graham Hodgett's notes taken from Leominster News dated Friday 14 January 1887 gives an insight into health care, to quote:-

"On Wednesday 29 December, an adjourned meeting was held in the schoolroom to make arrangements for the formation of a doctor's club, on the plan of a provident dispensary. The Vicar, Rev. W. E. Edwards, R.D. presided. At the previous meeting it was resolved to ask Howard D. Buss Esq. to attend and that gentleman was accordingly present. It was ultimately agreed upon, after some discussion, to adopt the doctor's terms, namely: four shillings per year per adult and one shilling per year for children below 16 years of age, to be paid quarterly in advance. The Committee will meet and consider a code of rules after which another public meeting will be called for their adoption. The club is open to the inhabitants of Orleton, Brimfield, Richards Castle, Bircher and the surrounding district. A surgery will be started in the village and a certain day each week will be appointed when the doctor will attend.

Mr. F. Fornear of the School, Orleton, was appointed secretary to receive contributions, and it was stated that from him all particulars might be had. It was also decided that medical attendance be ensured on payment of the first quarterly contribution."

Jumping many centuries forward, Kelly's Directory 1913 describes Orleton as "a village and parish on a loop of the Leominster and Ludlow road, which is also the direct road from Ludlow to Presteigne; 1½ miles from Woofferton Station on the Shrewsbury and Hereford (Great Western and London and North Western joint) railway, 5 miles south of Ludlow and 6 miles north of Leominster, in the northern division of the Wolphy hundred, Leominster Union, petty sessional and county court district; rural deanery of Leominster and archdeaconry and diocese of Hereford. The parish is 3 miles long and 2¾ miles wide. John Richard Hill who is Lord of the Manor, Edward Howarth Greenly Esq. of Titley, Mrs. Bright of Ludlow, Mrs. O'Conor, the Governors of Lucton School and Mrs. Yapp are the chief landowners ...... The chief crops are wheat, barley, beans, apples and hops. The area is 2,606 acres; rateable value £4,978; population in 1911, 584.

Post M.O. and T Office, - Albert Sidney James, sub post master. Letters arrive at 5.30am, delivered at 6.30am, dispatched at 7.45pm weekdays only.

Master of School - Edward Luther Stubbs. A.C.P.
Mistress   "   - Mrs. M. A. Stubbs.

PRIVATE RESIDENTS
Hill. Charles Samuel - The Laurels.
Hill. John Arthur - Kitchen Hill.
Hill. John Richard - Orleton Manor.
Johnson. James J. - Ashley Moor.
King. Rev. Eustice King. B.A. - The Rise (Spout House).
Munn. Rev. Joseph Shepherd (Vicar) - Vicarage.
Pudsey. Dawson - Towns End (Copper Corner).
Weaver. John Downes - Hemel Wall.

COMMERCIAL
Ancient Order of Foresters (Court Moor Park) Richard Passey (Sec) at Boot Inn.
Bedford. Martha (Mrs.) beer retailer - Bay Horse.
Bubb. Charles, farmer - Cullis Lodge.
Bufton. Chas, Cottage farmer - Common.
Davies. Josiah, farmer - Ashley Moor.
Evans. Arthur Thomas, farmer - Wood Farm, Orleton Common.
Griffiths. Benjamin, beer retailer.
Griffiths. George, farmer, hop grower.
Hall. John Minton, farmer, - Marsh Hall.
Herbert. William, farmer - Church House Farm.
Hill. John Richard, farmer and hop grower - Orleton Manor.
Holt. John, blacksmith - The Forge.
Hughes. Joseph, wheelwright - The Maidenhead.
Hughson. Samuel, cottage farmer - Colley Stocken.
Independent Order of Odd Fellows (James Price, sec) Maidenhead Inn.
James. Albert, Sidney, grocer - Post Office.
James. William, Edwin, farmer - Overton.
Johnson. James, agent to Mrs. O'Conor, Ashley Moor.
Jones. William, boot maker.
Lloyd. Thomas, farmer - Portway.
Maund. Thomas, shopkeeper.

Passey. Henry William, shoe maker.
Pearce. John, carpenter and - Maidenhead Inn.
Price. John, stone mason - Church Lane.
Price. Mary Ann (Mrs.), farmer - Lower House.
Price. Philip, cottage farmer - Green Lane.
Proctor. Thos. Hy, farmer - Cullis Lodge.
Saunders. Ann (Mrs.), farmer.
Saunders. Samuel, farmer, assistant overseer and Clerk to Orleton Parish Council.
Vale. Henry, cottage farmer - Orleton Common.
Vaughan. Henry, miller (water) - Orleton Mill.
Wall. Sarah (Mrs.), carrier.
Weaver. George, farmer - White House.

COMBERTON
Briggs. William, cottage farmer.
Edwards. Thomas, farmer.
Jones. Walter, farmer.
Smith. John, carrier.

Police Station, Henry John Luckett, Constable in Charge.
Carriers:- To Leominster, Mrs. Sarah Wall - Friday.
            Ludlow, John Smith - Saturday. Mrs. Sarah Wall - Monday and Saturday.

1941 Kelly's Directory

PRIVATE RESIDENTS
Faraday. Miss, - Church Croft.
Greenhaugh. Capt. Arthur, B.W.M.C. - Waterloo.
Hill. Lt. Col. John, Arthur, O.B.E., J.P. - Orleton Manor.
Hill. Miss, E. M. - Kitchen Hill.
King-King, Kenneth - Spout House.
Lewis, Rev. David William, B.A. (Vicar) - The Vicarage.
O'Conor. Charles, W. - Ashley Moor.
Weaver. (Mrs.) Marion - Hewell.

COMMERCIAL
Ancient Order of Foresters - George Parton (Sec) Boot Inn.
Apperley. Fred, farmer - Church House Farm.
Apperley. Geo., Alfred, farmer - Temple House.
Bedford. Mrs. Nellie - Bay Horse Inn.
Bennett. Richard, blacksmith.
Brick. Joseph, William - Cullis Lodge.
Bufton. Richard, smallholder - Woodcock Hall.
Cleaton. Wm. T. H., smallholder, Church Farm.
Davies. R., smallholder - Cullis Stocking.
Edwards. Kenneth, farmer - Inchmoor.
Evans. Harry Arthur, smallholder - The View. Orleton Common.
Gale. James, Henry, - Boot Inn.
Gittings. Hopton (Mrs.), shopkeeper.
Good. Cecil, Edward, farmer - Hewell Farm.
Griffiths. Ernest, farmer - Wood Farm, Orleton Common.

Griffiths. Harry, farmer - Little Waterloo.

Grosvenor. Harold, Hubert, farmer - White House.

Grosvenor. Mary, Ann (Miss), smallholder - Cullis Croft.

Hill. Lt. Col. John, Arthur, O.B.E., J.P., farmer - Orleton Manor.

Holland. Thos. J., farmer - Broad Green Farm.

Holt. R., Motor omnibus proprietor.

Independent Order of Odd Fellows (Jas. Price, Sec) Maidenhead Inn.

Ingram. Charles, farmer - Lower House.

Jones. Mrs. and Sons, farmers - Lodge Farm.

Jones. Ernest Geo., bootmaker - (next to the Old School).

Lloyd. Alfred, William, smallholder - Fairfield.

Maidenhead Inn. (Alfred, William Stephens).

Martins. Arthur, Vincent, smallholder - Little Folly
    (Clerk to the Orleton Parish Council).

Millichamp. George, Henry, grocer, provision merchant, tobacconist, corn, flour
    merchant and potato merchant - The Stores (Eagle House).

Morris. Ernest, farmer - Liners Farm.

Nicholls. Alfred, farmer - Overton Farm.

Passey. Harry, William, boot repairer - (Tunnel Lane, Bower Orchard Field).

Postons. Harry, wheelwright.

Pound. Samuel, farmer - Low, Tower Hill.

Powis. Arthur, Thos., newsagent - Green Lane.

Poyner. Ernest, farmer - The Farm.

Price. James, stone mason.

Price. Laura (Miss), smallholder.

Price. Philip, cottage farmer - Woodside.

Radnor. William, Edward, smallholder - The Folly.

Roberts. Jane (Mrs.), farmer - Marsh Hall.

Sparey. James, Michael, farmer - Portway.

Tarbath. Annie E. (Mrs.), smallholder - Upper House.

Thomas. Lilian (Mrs.), smallholder - Little Rise.

Thomas. William, smallholder - Whitestones.

Vale. Henry, cottage farmer - Orleton Common.

Vaughan. Albert, baker (Vaughan Bros.) - Ye Olde House.

Vaughan. Capt. Douglas, Cyril, M.R.C.S.Eng.L.R.C.P. Lond. physcn. and surgn.
    (attends Mon and Thurs).

Williams. Annie, Dorothy (Mrs.), farmer - Ashley Moor.

Post Office. M.O. and T.

Police Station.

COMBERTON

Martineau. Esmond, Savile - The Laurels.

Griffiths. Edward, farmer - Comberton House.

Grosvenor. Edwin, Chas., farmer.

Smith. A. Sybil (Mrs.), farmer.

Yarnold. Edith, Mary (Mrs.), smallholder.

Some of our photographs were produced at about the time the 1913 Kelly's was published and as expected they include farming and hop growing.

Arthur Mees's 1938 edition of Hereford says 'We remember Orleton for its old black and white houses grouped around a space where four roads meet.' We're more than pleased that readers will be able to recognise many existing properties from this collection. 1941 Kelly's continues to list a preponderance of farmers. There remains a police-station, blacksmith, 2 shop keepers, 2 boot repairers, newsagent, stonemason, baker, wheelwright, 1 omnibus proprietor (we've tried so hard to find a photograph of his bus) and a doctor's surgery for two days a week.

However the large part of our collection and notes are from local families and our own experiences. Ann was born at Inchmoor in the 1930s and attended the village school. We purchased Bower House in 1963 and it has been our home ever since. At that time the Boot landlord was Mr. David Gamble.

The Maidenhead - Mr. A. Stephens.
The Bay Horse - Mr. Jack Bowen.
The Post Office and Stores - Post master Mr. H. Drummond (the premises was only half its present size; the other half was a cottage).
General Stores - Ye Olde House - Mrs. Annie Vaughan. She was well known for her ice cream.
Baker - Mr. Ern Heapey.
Milk deliveries - Mr. Sid. Nicholls (Little Overton). He was known as one gear Sid because of his method of driving.
Mail delivery - Mrs. Phyllis Nicholls.
Coal Merchant - Mr. Jack Bowen and son John (Bay Horse).
Daily newspaper deliveries - Mr. Bill Preece (Hewell Cott.).
Sunday Newspapers - Mr. Tom Dyer (Green Lane, Namanga).

Cobbler - Mr. Ernie Jones (Rose Cottage, next to the Old School). Mr. Jones was 83; he cycled to Leominster every week. He was also the Verger and rang all three bells by himself by putting a foot in a loop of a bell rope (the loop is still there).

Wonderfully, mains water had just been laid through the village but many still carried their requirements from Dicken's Lane, Hallett's Well and other cluster wells.

The Headteacher of Orleton C of E School was Mr. Geoff Butcher. Children were taught up to the age of 11, then transferred to the new Wigmore High School.

"Plans are now in hand for the erection of a new school at Orleton which will also accommodate children from other villages".

The Parish room was still situated on the main Ludlow to Leominster road. It was an ex-army hut erected after the 1914-1918 War. There was no car park but traffic was quiet enough to allow parking on the road side.

"Efforts are being made to raise sufficient funds to build a new hall. Having acquired the land recently the necessary arrangements are being made for planning, purchase and erection of a new Parish Hall. The new site will also provide an adequate car park."

Woofferton Station was still open and very active. There were 155 dwelling houses in the area and 85 were without a fixed bath and water closet.

There were 341 on the electoral roll and 7 Parish Councillors. They were Mr. Fred Apperley, Mr. R. R. Worthing, Mr. David Williams, Mr. Reg. Grosvenor, Rev. J. T. V. Jones, Mr. Bert Fortey and Mr. J. M. Sparey. The Clerk was Mr. A. Jenkins (salary £5 per annum).

Meetings were at the school.

Mr. R. R. Worthing was the District Councillor (Spout House) and had represented the area continuously since 1951.

The Rev. J. T. V. Jones was vicar of Orleton and Brimfield.

Sister Hilda Bunce was the Methodist Circuit Deaconess.

The Boot Inn was well known for its duck suppers and samples from the menu are as follows:-

Prawn Cocktail - 4/6
Grapefruit - 1/6
Smoked Salmon - 5/6 (27½p)
Baked eggs - 1/6
Scampi - 5/6

Soup 1/6 - (7½p)
Corn on the Cob - 3/-
Potted shrimps - 4/6
Fruit Juice - 1/6

- -

½ Roast Duckling, sage and onion stuffing, roast potatoes and peas - 15/- (75p)
½ Roast Chicken, stuffing, roast potatoes, bread sauce and peas - 12/6 (62½p)
Grilled Steak, tomato, mushrooms, sausage, chips and peas - 12/6
Grilled ham, tomato, mushrooms, sausage, chips with one or two eggs - 10/6 (52½p)
Coq au Vin with rice - 17/6 (87½p)
Fresh Wye Salmon (when in season) new potatoes and parsley sauce - 10/6.

"It will surprise many to hear that a cattle market was held annually on 23 April (St. George's Day. Mr. Ingram tells me that it took place in the triangle of land in front of the lower churchyard gate. That would be opposite the village school of that time...."

(Extract from an article by Mr. George Platt in April 1980 Grapevine).

The layout of Orleton Properties had remained pretty well the same as the sketch map, for many years. The only additions were The Halletts in the 1940s, Green Lane Council Houses in the 1950s and St. George's Crescent during the early 1960s. Parish Council began to dispose of its Charity Land responsibilities and separate trustees were appointed for 'Orleton Relief in Need Charities' at the suggestion of The Charity Commission. Parish Council worked continuously to obtain a comprehensive mains sewerage and water scheme for Orleton. As a result of tremendous efforts by Councillor Mr. Reg. Worthing the District Council agreed to supply these amenities on one condition, that being, "to enable us to recoup our investment the community must allow us to develop properties along the lines of these proposed amenities within the village". The Parish Council and community realised that this would result in considerable change and development, but agreed in order to obtain modern amenities.

The District Council promised that plots would be gradually released over many years and a variety of properties individually and tastefully designed would be encouraged.

The laying of the sewerage system caused tremendous disruption with trenches 15 feet deep in places winding along our lanes. When the scheme was completed a junction was provided to those properties whose owners requested at a cost of £8 (a good week's wages in the early 60s).

An overall plan was produced to alleviate flooding. The brook was to be re-routed in places. The Ford was a constant problem and was bridged as a first stage, but land was sold, made available and development began much more rapidly and uniformly than expected. The flooding scheme was shelved because some properties were built on proposed deviations. Scores of damson trees were removed as well as a considerable amount of hedging. Numerous, similar properties sprung up. They looked so out of place and stark with the open unestablished spaces around them. Farmers tried to continue, as had always been their practice, to move their stock from one part of the village to another, but with the lack of gates and hedges many new lawns were disturbed. This of course persuaded many new occupants to modify the open plan and place boundaries around their properties.

There was much controversy about the erection of signs naming roads. It was argued that this was yet another step towards suburbia, but of course they were necessary to assist deliveries. As soon as the gleaming signs were erected they were blocked out with black paint. However our superb, local police constable reacted in his usual, quiet, effective manner. He patrolled our village late at night and on one occasion spotted a gentleman carrying some tomato plants in a box at about 2 a.m. He approached the gentleman and said, "Nice tomato plants you've got there". At the same time he looked into the box and saw a pot of black paint and a brush. Needless to say everyone got to know about this and the problem ceased. I'm sure the retired constable will recall the incident clearly. He always had his ear to the ground, knew everyone and was very effective.

Our new Village Hall was built with excellent parking facilities. After much negotiation between Parish Councillor Mr. Dennis Aldridge of Hewell and myself, an agreement was made with the late Mr. Fred Apperley for the Community to use part of the field next to the Hall for recreational facilities. For this wonderful opportunity Mr. Apperley asked only £5 per year. Eventually he sold the present Recreation Ground to Parish Council for £22,000, thus providing a superb, central amenity for future generations.

A new school was completed for our growing population in 1968, at a cost of £40,000, and Mr. Butcher was thrilled to move into modern facilities at last. The Little Hereford and Brimfield schools were closed - sad times for these two villages. Mr. Butcher had the very difficult task of absorbing their pupils and parents; but he was extremely sensitive and conscious of their anxieties and he and his staff did a splendid job to make them feel at home.

Our village has continued to develop and thrive. It remains a wonderful community in which to live, providing facilities for young and old alike. In fact one elderly gentleman said to the Rev. Peter Walter, "As far as I'm concerned, Orleton is the next best place to Paradise."

Ann and I feel that Orleton has been a model for the bonding of the indigenous population with the new. Many have made great efforts to support, become a part of and contribute to Orleton so ensuring a vibrant, lively community for us all to enjoy.

Orleton Houses 1940s

1	Little Folly	41	Village P.O., Stores and Corner Cottage
2	Bayhorse Inn	42	Bank House
3	The Folly	43	Bank Cottages
4	Comberton House	44	The Forge
5	The Cottage	45	Methodist Chapel
6	Comberton Cottages	46	Chapel Terrace
7	The Laurels	47	Brick Corner
8	Comberton Farm	48	Eagle House
9	Pool Cottage	49	Ye Olde House
10	Manor Cottage	50	Well Cottages
11	Poulters Cottage	51	Eagle Cottages
12	New House	52	Number 1 and 2 The Bower
13	Portway	53	Bower House and Bower Cottage
14	Portway Cottage	54	Number 1 Church Lane
15	Parish Room	55	Homeleigh
16	Fairfield	56	Stone House
17	Hope Cottage	57	No 1 Cottage and No 2 Cottage Church Lane
18	Tower Hill	58	Orchard Cottage
19	Sunnyside	59	Churchyard Cottage
20	Stone Cottage Green Lane	60	St. George's Church
21	Stone Cottage Green Lane	61	Vicarage
22	Broad Green	62	Church Croft
23	Lower Tower Hill	63	Unknown (Demolished)
24	Maidenhead Inn	64	Chapel House
25	Perseverance Cottage	65	The Boot Inn
26	Temple House	66	Upper House
27	The Police House	67	Lower House
28	The Mill	68	Woodcote
29	Millbrook Cottage	69	Church Farm
30	Millbrook House	70	Church Farm Cottage
31	Ford House and Ford Cottage	71	Claremont
32	The Cottage	72	Rose Cottage
33	The Farm	73	School
34	Townsend	74	Hernscott
35	Kitchen Hill	75	Halletts Well Cottages
36	Overton House	76	The Halletts
37	The Bungalow	77	Tunnel Lane Cottage
38	Little Overton	78	Hewell Cottage
39	Croft End	79	Hewell Farm
40	Orleton Manor	80	Brook Cottage

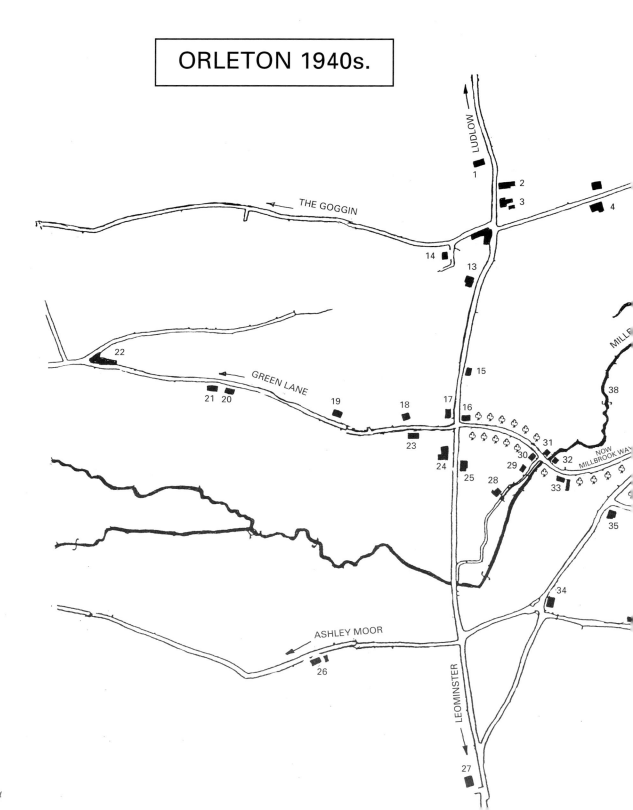

ORLETON 1940s.

LUDLOW

THE GOGGIN

GREEN LANE

NOW MILLBROOK WA

MILL

ASHLEY MOOR

LEOMINSTER

1
2
3
4
14
13
22
21 20
19
18
17
16
15
38
31
30
32
29
23
24
25
28
33
35
34
26
27

WOOFFERTON

CANAL

TUNNEL LANE

CANAL

Houses

Church Yard Cottage

    This property standing at the North end of Church Lane is one of the few cottages in the village that has not been recently modernised. It was built about 1640-1650 but at the beginning of the 19th century the front wall was moved out and the roof tiled, having formerly been thatched. The timbers are exposed on the Northern elevation.

    At the rear of the property there is the remains of a single cell property, which would have at one time been occupied by a farm worker and his family. (notes obtained 1989).

Orchard Cottage

"The Cottage which now has a galvanised roof was built about 1640 and would have been two rooms on each floor, an extension having been made perhaps about a 100 years later. An interesting feature is that in the ground floor room of the extension a large bread oven can be found taking up a considerable amount of floor space. A close examination of the construction of the roof shows that at one time it was thatched, the original pitch having been much steeper than the present day one. On the inside of the galvanised roof a layer of news-papers dated 1890s is in evidence and no doubt was an early form of insulation. Internally there is only one staircase to the upper parts and access to the other bedrooms is through another bedroom " (notes obtained 1989).

Orchard Cottage was modernised in 1993 by the village builders P. H. Postons and Son.

Church Lane Pre - 1950s

On the left can be seen numbers 1 and 2 Church Lane (now The Cottage), formerly agricultural workers' dwellings. The accommodation was very limited because the large wing to the rear was only added in the early 1980s.

Roman numerals can be seen carved in the timbers showing their original use was probably elsewhere. Wedging slots can be seen on the roadside elevation. These were used to raise the framework into a vertical position when the house was being built.

Many horseshoes have been found in the garden substantiating the opinion that this may well have been the site of the Manor stableyard. Further along to the left is Holmleigh (Bower Orchard) and The Forge faces the lane at the end. The cottage on the right has disappeared as has the wooden building at the top of Dicken's Lane.

CHURCH LANE, ORLETON.

Church Lane

Well Cottages near right. Eagle Cottages far right. The Forge in the distance and the black and white cottage on the Bower. The Woolaway bungalow has not yet been built.

Part of Church Lane 1964

The black and white cottages on the far right were until the 1970s the homes of the Deakin Family and Mr. Joe Vale the Boot barman. They have been converted into one property.

Middle right:- Stone House being renovated.

Near Right:- Holmleigh, re-named Bower Orchard in 1996.

Left are Nos. 1 and 2 Well Cottages (now one property) converted in 1992. The late Mrs. George an occupant of one of the cottages can be seen looking at Stone House.

Looking at the Glebe Land from Orchard View (Church Lane) with the old perry trees still standing and no houses. Miss Faraday's (Church Croft) in the background.

Church Lane 1970
The Woolaway bungalow on the right had recently been built.

Church Lane viewed from Wesleyan Chapel 1920s. On the right is No. 1 Church Lane and Holmleigh (Bower Orchard) in the distance. On the left Eagle Cottages. The gaggle of geese sitting on the grass island look unlikely to be disturbed by traffic.

The Forge

This was known as The Smith's Shop. For many generations it was used for blacksmith general repair work, wrought iron work and farriery.

In 1891 William Newman was the resident blacksmith.

He was followed by John Radnor. Then Mr. Holt. (Many of you knew him and may certainly have seen him singing in the Craven Arms Mens' Chorus until the late 1970's).

Mr. Holt was followed by Mr. Francis. When he retired, the work was continued by a 'travelling' blacksmith, Mr. Bennett from Bircher. The Smith's Shop closed when Mr. Bennett retired in 1945, the reasons being there was no-one locally to take the work on and increased mechanisation after the war reduced farrier demand.

In the 1930s Mr. Alf Sparey used to take horses regularly from Portway farm to be shod at The Forge. He and his brothers would tie the horses to Colonel Hill's rickyard gate. They then walked to the Forge to see how many horses were in the queue waiting. Occasionally the number waiting was considerable in which case the blacksmith would shoe the Portway horses later in the day, tie them up at the rickyard gate again and the boys would collect them on their way home from school. Once a month the boys continued on to the Manor. Here Mrs. Hill would be sitting behind a large table collecting childrens' savings. When sufficient was collected by each individual she would transfer it to National Savings for them.

The Manor farm barn which was taken down in the late 1980s. In the foreground is the gateway referred to by Mr. Alf Sparey.

Brick Corner House

Extract from 'Herefordshire - Historical Monuments 1939. Royal Commission on Historical Monuments':-

"Brick Corner, cottage, was largely rebuilt in 1728 - condition - poor."

Dating back to the seventeenth century a cottage built on a stone base, cellar under one section of the building and half timbering to the upper portion, some of the original remains today. In 1728 the property was largely rebuilt using handmade bricks that probably were made locally. The bricks used on the outer facing of the house are the small handmade type in a whole brick form whereas the internal parts of the walls are constructed from the half and broken bricks and rubble. The walls are solid, being between 18″ and 22″ thick with no cavity, the whole built on the original stone base.

A plaque on the West facing elevation gives the date 1728 and the initials "WMM" which may have been the owners or indeed builders at that time. On the gable end facing the North two sandstone heads appear, one of which is mostly intact except for the hole bored in it by some uncaring builder eager to fix an overflow to a toilet. The other face had completely disappeared and in 1983 an amusing builder moulded the monkey face!

In the nineteenth century the property was divided into two farm workers' cottages and on the rear of both properties kitchen extensions were added over the years. At one time on the Southern gable end a doorway was used with a timber staircase to it and this gave access to the room in which the cider was consumed as the property was at one time a cider outlet. This doorway has now been replaced by a window.

Since 1981 the house has been renovated, the kitchen extensions removed and the property returned to one dwelling, the original doorways being used and many old features exposed. Unfortunately the bake-oven was lost with one of the kitchen extensions although evidence exists in the Inglenook.

In the early 1990s a kitchen extension was added by P. H. Postons and Son when the property was the home of Mr. Jimmy Jack and family.

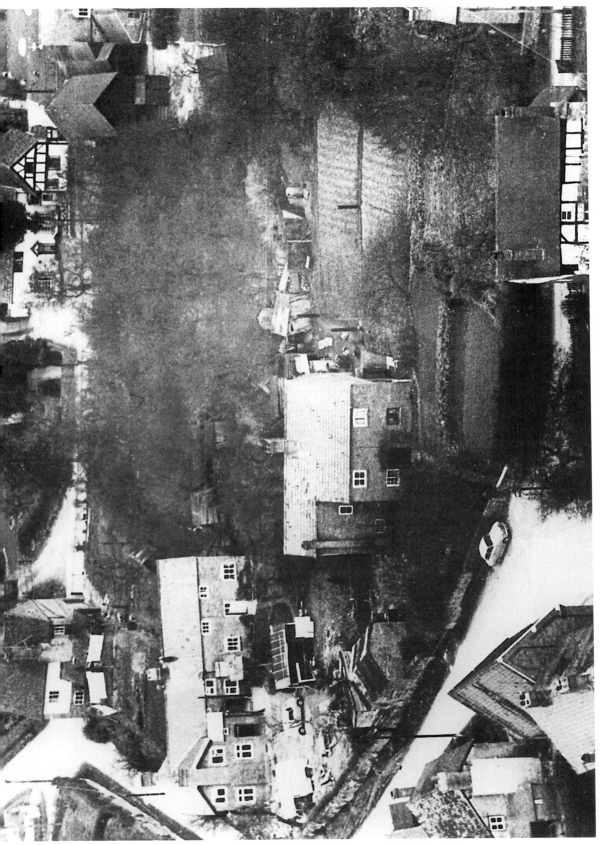

Brick Corner and The Bower.

Bower House/Cottage

In the early 1800s Bower House was an implement shed, Bower Cottage a cider mill, Brick Corner farm workers' cottages and The Bower (the property opposite the Chapel) was the farm house. Bower House front lawns and soft fruit area was the farm foldyard and Bower Cottage vegetable garden was a large farmyard pool. It is clearly shown on the 1860s parish map.

The implement shed had a rear wall of stone and wooden roof supported by wooden stanchions at the front. If you walk round the rear of Bower House the original stone wall can be distinguished quite clearly.

In the mid 1800s this wall was raised to its present height and the remainder of a new house built in brick. On the roadside the lounge and bedroom above had bay windows. Since being a house the property has been used as a private dwelling, a surgery and a police station. To the rear of the house one of the cell windows still remains. In the 1960s the house was condemned. The roots of a large ash tree had penetrated to the middle of the dining room and cracked exterior walls from roof to ground level. In 1964 the present owners renovated and modernised the house. The Cider Mill was converted to a cottage in the early 1900s but signs of its original use can still be seen around the property. The pulping stone stands outside Bower House, the troughing and cheese stone form part of the garden rockery and the cheese stone base and channel can be seen at the entrance to Bower Cottage.

In the 1980s Mr. Jenkins and his son Graham completely redesigned and renovated Bower Cottage interior. In the process they took up the old tiled floors and while removing earth beneath discovered a complete donkey's skeleton. They believe it could have been the animal used to operate the pulping stone.

Number 1 and 2 now known as The Bower

Until the late 1960s this was two dwellings known as Number 1 and 2 The Bower. Mr. Sidney Vaughan (locally known as Sooty because of his occupation) lived in the left hand side looking at the photograph and Mr. and Mrs. Bill Powell lived in the right side. A well in the garden was the official water supply for these dwellings, Bower House and Bower Cottage. Mr. Passey owned Numbers 1 and 2 and also the damson orchard which ran from the rear of the properties down to the Boot Inn. Mr. Brian Cade purchased the Cottages in the late 1960s and local builder, Mr. P. Postons converted them into one dwelling. In the 1970s Timbercroft was built on the damson orchard opposite The Boot Inn.

Orleton Manor
A more unusual view from the eastern side

Orleton Manor

The coppice opposite used to be a plum orchard with a tremendous variety of plum trees. We are told that it was the pride and joy of Col. Hill.

Orleton Manor

'Extract from Herefordshire Historic Monuments 1939'. "A timber framed residence of two storeys with cellars and attics and having a slate covered roof was probably built in the late 16th century. It was built on a half H-shaped plan with wings extending towards the South East. There is a modern addition to the South West elevation. The fairly close-set timber framing is mostly exposed and the house retains much of its original appearance. Inside the building there are some original moulded ceiling beams.

The Manor of Orleton (spelt Alretune in Domesday Book) was given by William The Conqueror to Ralph de Mortimer. After the death of Edward IV it became and remained the property of the Crown until 1609 when it was conveyed to George Hopton by James I. He then in turn transferred it to Messrs. Curteen, Warner and Wilton, who conveyed it to John Popham. After he died his brother, Alexander Popham, sold it to Thomas Blount, the famous Antiquary, who was a member of one of the most ancient families in England. At this time poet Pope visited the Manor because he was in love with Miss Martha Blount (The Encyclopaedia Brittanica confirms this).

The property was eventually in the hands of Archibold Blount when in 1860 a Mrs. Hill took the property and when Archibold died the Hills bought it outright and owned it until 1984/5. In 1825 the sale particulars showed the whole of the Manor to be 2,500 acres. In 1892 The Manor was also called Orleton Court and Court House. In the 'State' room the following inscription is cut into the stone mantle; "Honner Him in Hart that Souffered on the Crosse for THEE and Worship Him."

A cannonball was discovered embedded in the wall when the main staircase was replaced in the last century. Various sources describe the stay of Charles II at Orleton Manor following the battle of Worcester in 1651.

Several examples of carving by Alice Hill are to be found in the house, along with a magnificent carved bed, weighing about ⅓ of a ton, standing 8ft high and having been twice extended in length, which was carved in 1896 by the aforesaid AMH. The inscription;- 'AMH - DEUS - LUX - MEA - QUEM - TIMEBO? - 1896' (GOD IS MY LIGHT - WHOM SHALL I FEAR?)

She was partnered by JH, according to the headboard, presumably the John Richard Hill who was the leasee of the Manor at the time it was sold by Yale University, following the death of Archibald Henry Blount, who died without issue in 1907. It was on the advice of Sir Arthur Conan Doyle that the Manor was sold and that Blount's relatives be presented with the proceeds.

A carved fire surround in the dining hall is inscribed:-

'Whate'er events betyde, t'is wisdom times them alle'

The Royal Commission on Historical Monuments in Herefordshire Vol. III describes the 1934 listing, and interestingly describes the North Porch as previously being a bay window. As it was no doubt built as a porch, it became a bay, then a porch (in 1891 and 1934) and is now a bay again. The window in the North-west gable was not then visible and the third window has been restored to the bay above the main porch more recently into the original mullions. The panelling in the N.E. wing is 17th Century with a carved frieze and its condition is good.

The Lordship of the Manor which is transferred with the Manor House, had the last published reference in 1914 when Richard Hill was recorded as Lord of the Manor. Colonel Hill sold the Manor to Robert and Emily Jones in 1985 who started a hand painted tile business from the barns. The Manor was acquired by Chris and Sue Marsden on 6th January 1994.

Claremont - Kings Road

The red brick front section of this house was constructed on this site in the 1850's by the Price family and was occupied by the same family until the early 1960's. Beneath this part of the house a cellar from an earlier date is to be found which would indicate originally a much earlier property.

The barn at the rear of the property was constructed at three different times as can be seen from the change in the roof lines.

Our photographs of 1925 show Orleton Band and the May Queen procession. Edie Radnor was the May Queen - aged 10.

In those days Claremont was the village Post Office. The photograph shows a lean-to structure at the rear where the Post Office business was conducted. It remained as such until the present village stores became the Post Office in 1958, run by Mrs. Cotterill.

Like many local properties, Claremont had its own cider press.

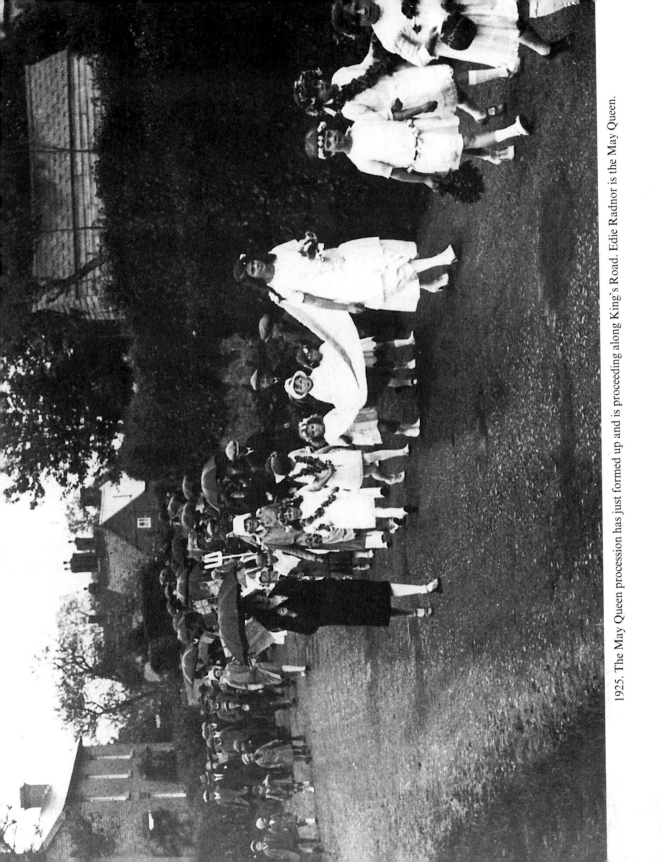

1925. The May Queen procession has just formed up and is proceeding along King's Road. Edie Radnor is the May Queen.

1925. May Queen procession returns through the village for crowning ceremony and Maypole dancing on Glebe Meadow.

The banner reads: LONG-LIFE HEALTH & HAPPINESS TO OUR MAY QUEEN

Outside the Old School, Orleton. Beattie and Joe Radnor ready to join the May Queen Parade 1925.

1925 Glebe Meadow. Crowned May Queen and attendants watching the Maypole dancing.

The Village, Orleton

Upper House near left.

Upper House

The house has a brick front which has now been rendered and pointed, with timber frame ends and rear. The theory is that a wealthy man had seen a similar house in one of the large cities but couldn't afford the expensive bricks for all the walls and consequently the front elevation was built with brick and the rest in a cheaper timber frame, all of which is reclaimed timbers.

As is so common in the village the stonework in the cellar of this house would suggest that it is of an earlier date than the house now standing above it.

There is evidence that it once had a stone tile roof, but the massive weight proved too much and cracked some of the roof trusses and a lighter clay tile was put on.

The house has been constructed in three apparent stages:- The main block parallel to the road, then the gable end at the rear which stands about 12″ clear of the front block but joined by the roof and thirdly the lean-to brick dairy.

It would appear from inscriptions which have been discovered on the plasterwork in the house that at one time this was an educational establishment. The rules of the school as illustrated in the photograph below are what have been uncovered. Unfortunately not all the rules of the school are readable but here are some that are:-

Sit where I bid you.

Come to school with decent books.

Pronounce your words "carefully"??

To mind your books when to play.

Also written over the door in the hall way

"When in school pray quiet be or else expect a whipping soon from me". Robert Cowper.

In the church records there is a reference to John and Mary Cowper and the births and deaths of some of their children around the 1700-1780 period. A reference is also made in a local history book of a village school being run by a master and his wife prior to the Victorian one opposite the church. Could this be the school referred to?

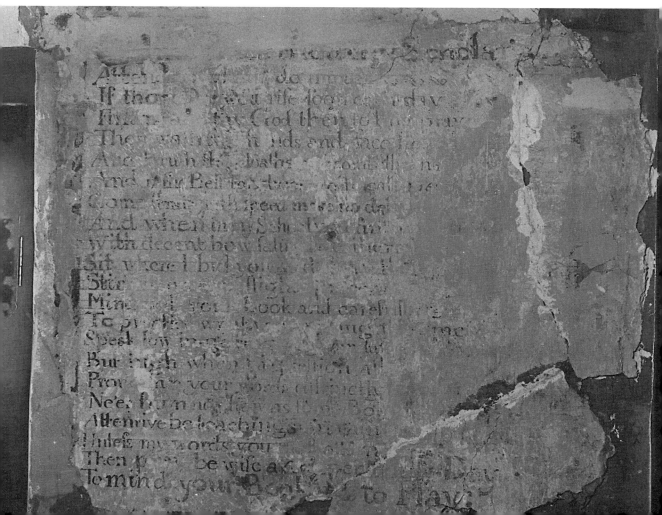

Orleton House

Lower House, Orleton (Orleton House)

"Leominster News" Series

Orleton House

From a publication called 'Historical Monuments', dated 1934, when the property was known as 'Lower House'.

"It is of T-shaped plan with the cross-wing at the S. E. end. In the middle of the S. E. front the upper storey projects and is gabled; the curved brackets spring from shaped shafts attached to the main posts. On the N. E. side is a projecting gabled dormer with moulded bressummers, brackets and barge-boards with an apex-post; the window is of four transomed lights with diamond-shaped mullions. A doorway on this side has a shaped head, and there is also an original window of four main transomed lights with moulded frame and mullions; below the sill is a shaped bracket. Inside the building are some original moulded ceiling-beams."

Orleton House in the 1930s was known as The Seven Gables. It is easy to see why from the photograph.

Looking from the roadside, to the right of the house is the entrance to an old fold yard. This 1934 photograph shows the property looking from the yard. To the right of the bay window is a black rectangular shape. There are residents in the village who remember this as a 'carriage way' which passed through the property.

In 1968 Dr. Vaughan made it Orleton's first permanent surgery. It later became the home of Dr. and Mrs. Snape and the surgery remained in part of the house until 1984. In the 'yard' there is an iron fireback with the initials and date F.B. 1630.

Ye Olde House

From 'Old Cottages, Farm Houses, etc. in Herefordshire'

Ye Olde House 'in the Main Street would be difficult to improve upon, unless one could call back the oriel window in the gable, where the solid moulded sill remains. The characteristic of the district again appears in the mingled stone and brick and flag slates. The side of the joists supporting the overhanging gable have been painted white with good effect.'

Mr. and Mrs. Vaughan bought the property in 1934 from the Postons family. Prior to this date it had been two properties. They made it into one. Looking at the property from the roadside the left hand side was made into the bakery and housed the bake ovens too. In 1958 Mr. Vaughan moved the bake ovens to the right hand side of the property. This enabled Mrs. Vaughan to convert the front half of the left side into a shop. She was well known particularly for her wool. The shop continued until 1973.

The baking ceased in 1960 when Mr. Vaughan died. The bake ovens were removed and Mr. and Mrs. Bradbury occupied the right side. The bakery became the shop store for wool etc. The brother of Mrs. Vaughan, Mr. Heapey, became the baker and his bakery is still opposite the church. When he left school he was trained in Ye Olde House by Mr. Vaughan - and a very good job he made of it too.

Prior to 1934 the Vaughans lived at the Mill (down the lane off Millbrook Way by the brook). Mr. Vaughan was the miller and his mother was the baker. They left The Mill because of a disastrous fire in 1934, and so we can say that the family have been bakers in this community for the best part of a century.

Col. Hill and Rev. J. T. V. Jones both claimed that Ye Olde House is the oldest property in the village. This is probably true. It is clearly a most picturesque building and undoubtedly has been sketched and painted more than any other in the village over the years.

"Ye Olde House"

Church Croft

It is difficult to recognise Church Croft from this old photograph because in the 1990s it is more secluded. The five barred gate and the building no longer exist. It has been the home of the Faradays for many years and in the 1940/50s members of their family held a private school there.

Kitchen Hill

A lovely view of this property taken in the 1940s, with the resplendent turkey oak on the left. We noticed that it was ½d to send the post card from which this copy was taken.

We are told that Kitchen Hill got its name because of troops establishing their kitchens at this position during the Civil War.

On the same side of the road at the end of the coppice area there remains an old nissan hut. Mr. David Williams and other Home Guard members said that this was where Colonel Hill stored much of their equipment.

Opposite page:

The Farm, Millbrook Way, taken in the 1920s from Kitchen Hill road near the site of the old oak tree. Note the oast houses and the thatched roof on the building next to the house.

Aerial view of The Farm, Millbrook Way, in the 1940s. The oast houses and thatched building have gone. On the far side of the lane cattle sheds and a dutch barn lead to orchards and Mill brook.

Barnside

Little more than 30 years ago Millbrook Way was a narrow lane with high hedges on either side, an abundance of damson trees and a ford. Barnside was the first 'new' property to be built in the Way. The land was purchased in 1967 and this property completed in 1969. It was called Barnside because of its proximity to the barn shown in the photograph.

Three months after Mrs. Bowen moved in there was a terrific flood which stretched to within a few feet of the War Memorial crossroads. The Cottage where Mrs. Betty Robinson now lives was badly flooded and with the help of a canoe Mr. A. Jenkins and Mr. D. Williams helped remove floating carpets and furniture. Looking from the opposite side of the road, where there used to be a raised, railed footpath, Barnside looked like Noah's Ark. It was completely surrounded by water but its substantial concrete foundation remained well above flood level.

The Farm Millbrook Way 1928
Edward John Morgan and Mary Mildred Morgan.

The Cottage, Mill Lane
1940s.

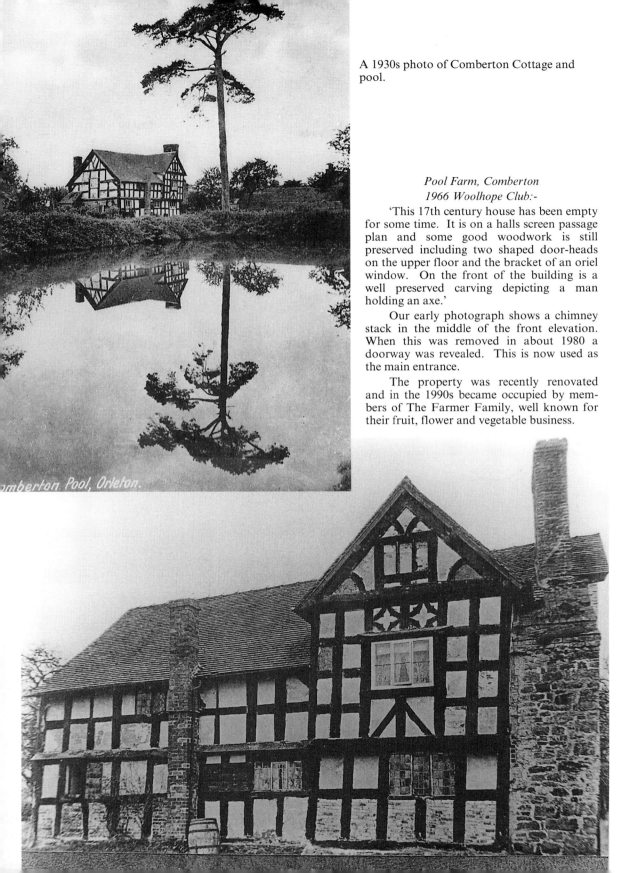

A 1930s photo of Comberton Cottage and pool.

Pool Farm, Comberton
1966 Woolhope Club:-

'This 17th century house has been empty for some time. It is on a halls screen passage plan and some good woodwork is still preserved including two shaped door-heads on the upper floor and the bracket of an oriel window. On the front of the building is a well preserved carving depicting a man holding an axe.'

Our early photograph shows a chimney stack in the middle of the front elevation. When this was removed in about 1980 a doorway was revealed. This is now used as the main entrance.

The property was recently renovated and in the 1990s became occupied by members of The Farmer Family, well known for their fruit, flower and vegetable business.

Comberton Pool, Orleton.

Aerial view of Comberton 1960s

This lovely view shows Pool Cottage on the left and Comberton Farmhouse and buildings on the right where the Grosvenor family have lived for most of the 20th century. Reg Grosvenor recently gave us the privilege of looking around this most interesting old house. Upstairs in the "Nursery" there are numerous ancient paintings on the old plaster and beams. Also the pre-Roman numeral markings tell us that this part of the property was built in the 1500s, making it one of the oldest buildings in the area.

Cider Mill Comberton Farm

In spite of the fact there were numerous cider houses in Orleton in the early part of the 20th Century most farms continued to make their own cider for their work force, harvesters and everyday consumption.

COMBERTON FARM, ORLETON.

Comberton Farm House
1983 Woolhope Club:-

'The house appears to have been built in three stages. The hall and cross wing being the earliest part, the lean-to service bay to the eastern end. Later the house was extended to the east and there was a brick addition to the wing in the early 19th century. The longitudinal beam in the main chamber over the hall is supported by a renaissance type bracket. However the main interest is the mural design in the chambers in the parlour wing, a rare survival. It is continued over plaster and timber alike and below the frieze is a floral pattern of six petalled flowers of various sizes which are best preserved on the door heads and posts. The colours used are red, blue, white and yellow. The pattern has been damaged by a number of layers of wallpaper.'

Little Folly was known as the Old Plough. It became a private house in the 1930s. It was modernised in the late 1980s and looks very different without its thatched roof.

The Folly

The Bay Horse   The Folly   Little Folly

The area in the 1890s was known as The Folly. All three properties were drinking houses. Most locals found it difficult to get past all three and remain sober - hence The Folly. The Radnor's property (The Folly in the 1990s) in the foreground was called The Plough. It was a cider house and the proprietor in the 1890s was Mr. J. Phillips. It remained as a public house until about 1907 when he became mentally ill. The sign was taken down but the pear tree in which it hung continued to stand by the main road until it was felled in 1953.

The Bay Horse was the last of the three properties to become a drinking house. Two retailers resided there in 1876. Mr. George Matthews was the cider retailer and Sarah Wall the beer retailer. In that year it was known as The Folly. Next door were the stables for the area as a result the public house was given the name The Bay Horse in the 1930s. The Plough became The Folly and the Old Plough Little Folly. The Bay Horse ceased to be a licenced property in 1974 when Jack and Ivy Bowen retired. Mr. Bowen was also the local coal merchant.

The Radnor Family

The Radnor Family has been associated with Orleton for nearly 200 years. During that time they have always been active in the community.

Edie's and Beattie's Great Grandfather William Radnor was a member of The Odd Fellows Society in 1828. Their Great Grandmother lived for some time at Church Croft (Miss R. Faraday's home in the 1990s). William's brother John was a recorded member of The Odd Fellows in 1826.

William's son, another William Radnor was an Orleton butcher. He lived at Lower Tower Hill (Stillwater Cottage in the 1990s). His son William Edward Radnor was born at Lower Tower Hill in 1870. In 1895 he married Margaret Jones who lived at The Old Plough (Little Folly). They moved to The Folly in 1912. It had been a cider house for many years. Edie born in 1915 and Beattie in 1916 were two of a family of nine children. William continued to rent land at Tower Hill until 1921 (home of Talbot and Dorothy Griffiths in the 1990s). During this year a considerable portion of Orleton Manor land was divided up and sold. We found one part of Tower Hill sale notice quite interesting namely:- "The Premises are Copyhold of the Manor of Orleton, and subject to a quit rent of 7d and a small heriot." The word heriot meant that on death or quitting the tenant's family would be asked to forfeit a prime beast or something else of value.

John Radnor had a son who lived at Waterloo. He helped to build Waterloo Chapel, while way back in 1830 Richard Radnor was mentioned in connection with Orleton Methodist Chapel.

Edie Radnor remained at The Folly until 1996 when due to ill health the property was put up for auction. Beattie reminded us at that time that the cider mill was still virtually in working order.

In true Radnor tradition Edie has been a very active participant of Orleton community. She was a regular member of St. George's choir in her younger days and worked tirelessly for the church as long as the authors can remember. Her contribution to WI was considerable. In May 1965 she was chosen to represent the group at a special Royal Garden Party at Buckingham Palace. She loved to participate in WI entertainment and was a real star organising games at past joint YFC and WI Christmas parties. Lately of course it has been impossible to think of Bingo at the Village Hall without her being financial overseer.

HEREFORDSHIRE.

PARISH AND MANOR OF ORLETON.

Desirable Brick-built Dwelling-House and Pasture Land.

MR. R. H. GEORGE

WILL SELL BY AUCTION,

AT THE ROYAL OAK HOTEL, LEOMINSTER,

On Friday, September 30th, 1921,

At **3** o'clock in the Afternoon punctually, subject to Conditions of Sale, the

Dwelling-House, with excellent Garden, Outbuildings, and Two Pieces of Pasture Land,

KNOWN AS

'Tower Hill,'

Situate in the Green Lane, Orleton, viz. :—

No. on Ordnance Map.	Description.	Quantity.
458 -	House, Buildings and Garden -	.535
459 -	Pasture -	1.147
460 -	Ditto -	1.158
	A. -	2.840

or **2 acres 3 roods 14 perches** (or thereabouts).

The House is brick and stone-built and slated, and contains Sitting Room, Kitchen, Larder, Back-Kitchen and 3 Bedrooms. The Outbuildings consist of Closed Shed, Barn and Cellar with tiled roofs. The House and part of the Garden are in the occupation of MISS WATKINS, **Vacant Possession of which will be given on the 25th March next.** The rest of the Premises are in the occupation of MR. W. E. RADNOR on a Lady-Day Tenancy. There is a Closed Shed in No. 459.

The Premises are Copyhold of the Manor of Orleton, and subject to a quit rent of 7d. and a small heriot.

The Tithe-rent Charge is 10s. 3d.

Further Particulars may be obtained from the Auctioneer, Croftmead, Kingsland, Herefordshire; or from **HENRY GOSLING, Esq., Solicitor, Leominster.**

Turnpike Cottage

When you next walk past Mr. and Mrs. Bowen's property 'Lendoma' towards The Knoll, have a look in the hedge. You will most likely see roses and other cultivated plants, apparently in the middle of nowhere. This was the site of Turnpike Cottage which was unfortunately demolished in the 1930s.

The Rise

The Rise in the 1920s. The home of Captain and Mrs. King-King. Captain King-King was the President of The Rabbit Club. He held an annual party for the members in the grounds. He often visited the Village Stores on horse back. The Youth Club had an annual outing to the sea-side and Captain King-King's one piece, striped bathing costume was a major attraction. The Rise is now The Spout House and in the 1990s is the home of the Worthing Family.

Every year Captain King-King went to the village school to judge the ten garden plots. He always presented the pupil who had obtained the best result with a new garden fork.

1930s. Marriage of Captain Kenneth King-King to Penelope Lines of Ashley Moor Hall - the joining of two well known Orleton families at St. George's. The photo includes Gerald Anson, a youthful John Evans, Bill and Charlie Ingram and one of the Carpenter boys.

School

School Reminiscences. Mrs. Joan Edwards (1924)

We always walked to school in a gang. Each family waited for others who came past their home, then they continued towards school together.

We all wore boots with lots of studs. We couldn't bear them because they were not lady-like and very heavy and we used to do our best to scuff the studs out - all to no avail because when we arrived home at night, our dad would inspect them and put more in. We all had to wear pinafores too to protect our clothes.

We carried our jam sandwiches in a metal box and shared the contents with other members of the family at lunch time. We were a big family and there was always a large pile of sandwiches prepared for us each morning. However those early in the queue took too many and the late comers had few.

There wasn't a drink to take to school only a bucket of water waiting there which had been carried from Hallett's Well. Everyone dipped a cup into the bucket. An old trick was to tell the Headmistress that someone had knocked the bucket over, by accident of course - then we would be sent to get more and waste lesson time. I never recall any facility for washing hands, not a pleasant thought when you remember that we had the old bucket toilets.

When the whistle blew in the mornings we lined up outside and marched into the big room all together for scripture. Afterwards we divided into three classes.

Heating was provided by two open coal fires and one black stove with a guard round it. If it was cold and wet we were allowed to stand round and warm ourselves.

Lessons were mainly reading , writing and arithmetic. In the middle class we had a large set of tables on the wall so we were able to glance up and obtain the correct answers. How we missed that chart when we moved to the big room and how apparent it became we had remembered little by rote.

Exercise was football down the lane in 'Mill Meadow'. We played in our ordinary clothes of course and the girls played just as hard as the boys. Mr. Barrow, the Headmistress's husband was our referee. Drill took place regularly on the playground and seemed mainly to be teaching us our right from our left.

In the bottom playground we were encouraged to share little plots of garden and grow flowers.

The Revd. Payne Brown came in at intervals to teach us scripture. When an inspector was due we were told all about it beforehand and warned to be extra specially well behaved and alert.

Our inkwells had to be filled regularly and the monitors often got in an awful mess.

Millbrook flooded regularly and occasionally prevented us from getting to school especially when water was swirling down the road from Broad Bridge to the Maidenhead.

Knitting lessons are vague in my mind but I do remember girls rolling wool and getting it in a real muddle.

I remember one of my brothers being ridiculed about spelling. The teacher said, "Your younger sister would be able to spell that." As a result I was sent for to demonstrate but instead I burst into tears.

The dentist was a dreaded visitor and many squeals and much crying was heard on that day; and of course the 'nit nurse' came regularly to inspect our heads for head lice.

There was always a celebration in the field on St. George's Day. We played a variety of games and received a sweet each. We had long desks with attached seats and six of us sat in a row. An inkwell was positioned in front of each of us. Books were given out as required because there was nowhere to keep them in the desk. This meant we had numerous monitors. Pencils and pens with nibs had to be issued and collected too.

I cannot recall any school outings but we always had a Christmas tea in the village hall where sticky buns suspended on strings were eaten and bobbing apples in buckets of water were competed for.

I found school basic, enjoyable but often very cold.

One boy used to bring a bottle of cider for his lunch drink. "We boys used to drink it between us and as a result laugh and giggle and be quite tiddly," reported Alf Sparey.

Memories of Orleton School 1945-50 by Ann Jenkins (nee Edwards)

I have happy memories of my school days at Orleton School. My Headteacher was Mrs. Price who lived in the school house. Her husband was a farmer who lived at Penybont so unfortunately they could only see each other at weekends. She had two children Betty and Peter. Peter was my age and in my class. He was not always very well behaved. Mrs. Price taught in the 'big room' which was heated by a tortoise stove. As this was fuelled with coke it was a slow burning stove. The room was very cold and draughty unless of course you were sitting very near to the heat and then it was almost too hot. Miss Yarnold was the infant teacher and she taught in the smaller room. She was very kind and gave strawberries and sweets for good work. When she retired her place was taken by Miss Millicent Morris (now Godding). She lived at the Lyners (near Goggin) and cycled to school. She was related to me so I thought she was "special". Another teacher was Miss Nora Apperley (Marsh). To me she seemed too young and too pretty to be a teacher.

The cookery room was used for the older childrens' craft lessons and for serving dinners. These were delivered in tins in a van and served by several dinner ladies. I can remember Mrs. Chadd, Mrs. Wall and Mrs. Carpenter serving and they washed the plates in the sink in the porch. Dinners cost 2s/1d about 10p per week. In inclement weather when the van couldn't get to school emergency rations were used. These were kept in the cupboard in the cookery room and included bovril, corned beef and dry ryvita type biscuits.

Drinking water was carried from Halletts Well (outside the present school) in a bucket on a stick by two pupils on a rota system. There were many times after struggling with a heavy bucket of fresh water that big lads would throw stones, soil or leaves into the bucket. The water would have to be tipped out and the struggle started all over again. What a waste of lesson time! The same mug was dipped into the bucket by each pupil if they wanted a drink.

The toilet block was across the playground. The buckets were emptied by Mr. Mapp. I always felt sorry for him as he was such a short man and the buckets seemed so big.

The toilet paper hanging on strings was ripped up sheets of news or other papers - nothing was wasted in those days.

I have vague memories of parading down the lane (between the old school and the bakery) to Mill Meadow behind someone carrying a flag - must have been a special day. Mill Meadow was used as a playing area but it was a boggy field and often too wet for anything. I can remember playing ball on the wall of the Old Vicarage opposite the school lane. The old playground wall was a favourite spot for climbing and sitting on and the old lane itself added extra space to the playground. It had a cinder base as all the coke ash from the stove was emptied there.

Older pupils played with younger ones. We played 'The Farmer's in his den', What's the time Mr. Wolf?' 'Here we come gathering nuts in May'. 'The wind, the wind, the wind blows high' - all singing rhymes with actions. We played hopscotch and many skipping games.

Monday was savings day when those with money to save walked from the school to the Post Office (Claremont) to buy stamps at 10d each. When a page of the savings was filled with 10d stamps a £1 certificate could be bought. This was good training for saving in later life.

Children walked or cycled to school. I walked from Inchmoor a trek of over a mile, later cycling on a small cycle and then cycling with my small sister riding on a bike seat while I pedalled. I was accompanied by three children from a nearby cottage who walked up the railway line to join me. If we dawdled and were late for school the others always told Mrs. Price it was my fault as I suffered from asthma; and they said I couldn't hurry. It was the school doctor who diagnosed the asthma. He said I would grow out of it and he was right.

Gardening was part of the curriculum especially for the big boys. Sewing also played a big part in school life. I started having migraine headaches at this time and blamed it on close-up needlework. I remember making a skirt and having to do three rows of small gathering stitches. It took many weeks to finish this work but when it was completed I took the skirt home to wear.

We sat in double desks in rows. When your partner wanted to lift the lid of the desk you had to move your books too whether you wanted to or not. My best friends at Orleton school were Joan Collings, Norah Lewis, Margaret Chadd, Dorothy Sheppard, Marie Griffiths and Audrey Powles. I was usually dressed in hand-me-downs, not very often anything new. But, I well remember when I had some new vests taking Norah in the toilet to show her. She must have been green with envy!!

This was the time of the 11+ examination. Some boys took this to enable them to go to Lucton School. If they passed the examination and were awarded the Pierrepoint Scholarship it enabled them to have free education at this fee paying school. Others sat for a scholarship to Leominster Grammar School. Free transport was available on the Midland Red bus from the Maidenhead. Others went to Kingsland School until the new High School was built at Wigmore. Mrs. Price was a good teacher, working hard and encouraging us to sit for these examinations.

Miss James (we called her Miss Religious James as she played the organ in church and helped with Sunday School) used to play the piano at school. She had a metronome on the top and she played with such vigour that occasionally this thing would vibrate off the piano and fly across the room. I remember Mr. Wickstead coming to play for dancing for the older children. He played the fiddle and used to dance around as he played it.

I enjoyed my time at Orleton School and was always very grateful to Mrs. Price and the other staff for preparing us for later life.

There was another school in Orleton at that time, at Church Croft and it was run by the Miss Faradays. We used to call it 'Faraday's College of Knowledge'. Only a handful of children went there. Their parents had to pay for their education.

Drawing of proposed Orleton School 1835 by Birmingham architect Mr. James Cranston.

Schoolhouse - Orleton.

Orleton School early 20th Century

Reported in the Hereford Times in 1854:-

The Foundation Stone of a New School at Orleton

"This public elementary school is to be of 14th century style in red brick with blue brick worked in crossings and bands and bath stone dressings to the windows and gables. It is to cost £1009 and accommodate 99 children. The roof will be of wrought open timber and covered with blue tiles in ornamental courses. The porches at the several entrances to the master's house and school rooms for boys and girls will be of wrought oak with arches. There will be tracery to the doorways and windows. The architect is Mr. Cranston of Birmingham (1st July, 1854)."

There was never any water supply and the last Headmaster, Mr. G. Butcher, carried lunch-time drinking water every day from the old vicarage.

'Cobbler' Jones, whose cobbler's shop was next door where Mr. and Mrs. Benson now reside, could be seen carrying water for other purposes to the school daily. This continued until the late 1960s. Perhaps someone still has Cobbler's yoke which helped him balance his buckets?

Parish Council meeetings were held in the school until it closed in December, 1967. Mr. Butcher and his staff moved to the new school in January, 1968, when it was opened by the Bishop of Hereford. Children from Brimfield and Little Hereford joined our Orleton pupils at Easter 1968.

Orleton School 1910-20. Showing the extension to the right known as the Cookery Room.

Orleton School 1907

Orleton School

Snippets from log books:

1922   Received notification that C. H. aged 13 has been granted a labour certificate for farm work. His name will be removed from the register.

Empire day. In the afternoon instead of the usual lessons I gave an address on 'Empire'. The children saluted the Flag, sang the National Anthem and other suitable songs.

1925   Miss M. away all day owing to a breakdown of her bicycle.

2nd June
School closed for May Fair.
School closed for three weeks by order of Chief Medical Offr. owing to increase in measles.

23rd June
Children returned. Only 20 present owing to prevalence of measles and whooping cough. Dr. Lowe advised closure until 2nd July.

30th July
Closed for Summer Holidays.

1926   The temperature is only 41° F at 9.00 a.m. Owing to General Strike there is no fuel.

1936   *13th November*
Little Hereford School has been burnt down this week. The fire began in the Infant Room chimney during the night and the whole school has been destroyed. All 36 pupils have been admitted to our school.

1939   *11th September*
Last Sunday, 3rd September, owing to the aggressiveness of Germany in confiscating the small countries of Mid-Europe, Britain and France declared war on Germany. Children from all large town areas have been evacuated. I have 20 on the register. I have managed to accommodate them and school carries on normally.

Early 1900s. Orleton School pupils.

Orleton School 1920s

1920s group at Orleton School

Back Row L to R:- Miss Jones, Mr. Stubbs, Mrs. Stubbs.
...............Williams, ...Edwards, Sid Edwards, Flossie Perks, Violet Parton, Rosemary Parton.

Middle Row:- Molly Handley, ...Brick, ...Brick, Winnie Hughson, Elsie Edwards, Reg Grosvenor.

Front Row: Alfie Palfrey, Edie Powles, ...

Orleton School 1929 Standards 1 and 3

Back Row L to R:- Sidney Edwards, Wilfred Matthews, Sidney Lloyd, ... Stanley Grosvenor, Jim Ingram,

Second Row:- Joan Sparey, Beattie Radnor, Annie Morris, Bill Sparey, Sam Hughson, Daisy Rogers, Enid Bowen, Kathleen Lamb.

Third Row:- Miss Bloom, Edie Radnor, Hilda Postons, ..., Violet Parton, Ivy Thomas, Nancy Martins, Evelyn Hughson, Ivy Rogers, Nancy Bufton, Mrs. Barrow.

Fourth Row:- Eileen Barrow, Winnie Williams, Marcia Price, Gwen Morris, Gladys Hodges, Agnes Maund, Joan Gittings, Nora Apperley, Ivy Passey, Bessie Chadd, Cecily Dyer, Naomi Williams, Francis Hill.

Front Row:- Lionel Moseley, Albert Jones, George Lamb, David Williams, Arthur Edwards, Tom Hill, Wilfred Vaughan.

Orleton 1930s
Back Row:- Bill Evans, Tom Hughson, Charlie Rawlings, Wilf Dallow, Albert Jones, Jack Sparey, Tom Apperley, Alf Sparey.
Front Row:- Hodges, Bob Brick, Dennis Rawlings, Stanley Rawlings, Derek Gale, Gilbert Powell, Bert Hill.

Orleton School 1930s
Back Row L to R. Nora Noble, Dennis Gittings, John Noble, Beryl Morris, Ethel Hill, Edie Morris, Jessie Evans, Hilda Gittings, Beattie Walters, Bob Brick, Bill Ingram, Bill Palmer.
3rd Row:- Eric Brick, Derek Gale, Vera Gale, Lill Wilcox, Barbara Collings, Phyllis Noble, Barbara Whitehurst, Joyce Vaughan, Bert Hill, Basil Bufton, Roger Williams, Charlie Walters.
2nd Row:- Maurice Carpenter, Sheila Morgan, Marg Collings, Dorothy Williams, Ruth Harris, Monica Bendall, Margaret Vaughan, Beryl Griffiths, May Bufton, Betty Price, Doris Griffiths, Hettie Sheppard, Sylvia Bowen, Eric Bridge, Raymond Carpenter.
Front Row:- George Wall, Trev. Shepherd, Charlie Ingram, Ken Postons, Talbot Griffiths.

A class at Orleton School 1932.

Back Row L to R:- Tom Hill, Wilf Vaughan, Jack Sparey, Roly Bradford, Wilf Matthews, Ben Edwards, Mrs. Barrow Headmistress.

Middle Row:- Bill Williams, Tom Davies, John Deeley, Tom Hughson, Cissie Dyer, Winnie Williams, Norah Apperley, Doug Bradford, Alf Sparey, Lionel Moseley.

Front Row:- Gladys Morris, Ivy Passey, Gladys Hodges, Joan Gittings, Phyllis Apperley, Betty Chadd, Margaret Holland.

Orleton School 1930s

Back Row L to R:- Mabel Hill, ..., ..., Mary Sparey, Freda Hill, Doris Thomas, Margaret Holland, Beryl Bridge, Ethel Hill.

Front Row:- Florrie Williams, Roger Williams, ..., Betty Price, Beryl Holland, Bert Hill, Alf Sparey, Eric Bridge.

Orleton School 1933

Back Row L to R:- ...., Tom Hughson, Cecil Griffiths, Margaret Holland, Ivy Passey, Cissy Dyer, Bessie Chadd, ..., Roland Bradford, Douglas Bradford, Bob Brick.

Middle Row:- Doris Thomas, ..., Beryl Holland, Doris Handley, Lil Wilcox, ..., ...,

Front Row:- ...., Eric Bridge? ...., ..., Arthur Postons?

Orleton School 1947

L to R:- Gary Duncalfe, Lionel Edwards, Raymond Duggan, Terry Smith, Ivy Thomas, Nigel Fuller, Marie Griffiths, ... Bufton, ..., ..., Derek Fortey, John Duggan, Valerie Edwards, ..., ..., Tom Sheppard, ... Lewis, Eileen Sheppard, Vic Ingram, John Brooks, Michael Ball, ..., Donald Wall, Cath Collings, ...,
Ida Bufton, Audrey Powles, Phyllis Bufton, Mary Lewis, Marion Jones, Ann Edwards, Glenys Shepherd, Joan Collings, Winnie Duggan, Marj Collings, ..., ..., Michael Sparey, Vera Wall, Dennis Edwards, Peter Price?, Mrs. Price.

Orleton School 1949

Back Row:- L to R Tommy Sheppard, Ivy Thomas, Eileen Sheppard, Ann Edwards, Mary Lewis, Pat Priday, ..., Jim Basham.

Middle Row:- Michael Heapey, Dorothy Sheppard, Raymond Duggan, Margaret Chadd, Norah Lewis, John Basham, Marie Griffiths, Nigel Fuller.

Front Row:- Michael Cork, Gary Duncalfe, Maureen Wall, Joan Collings, Pat Carpenter, John Brooks, John Lewis.

Orleton School 1950

Back Row:- L to R Miss Millicent Morris, Jean Fortey, ..., Terry Smith, Michael Sheppard, John Dyer.

Middle Row:- Gerald Jones, Geoffrey Kennett, Kathy Sheppard, Jean Underwood, Sally Sheppard, ..., Lionel Edwards.

Front Row:- Douglas Lowe, Eddie Lewis, Shirley Angell, Gill Edwards, Peter Brooks, Michael Wright.

Orleton School 1954

Back Row:- L to R Billy Burgoyne, David Wall, Dave Lewis, Les Bufton, Lionel Edwards, Mike Sheppard, Gary Duncalfe, Doug Lowe, Gerald Jones, ..., John Walters.

Third Row:- Mrs. Price, Janet Jones, Chris Phillips, Shirley Angell, Margaret Evans, Jean Underwood, Maureen Wall, Pat Carpenter, Sally Sheppard, Jean Fortey, Gill Edwards, Doris Phillips, Kathy Sheppard, Marg. Cooper, Miss Clarke.

Second Row:- Pauline Bloom, Pearl Mantle, Anthea Lowe, ..., ..., Doreen Kennett, Rosemary Underwood, Elizabeth Cork, Barbara Wall, Pat Edwards, Margaret Gittings.

Front Row:- Francis Jones, Chris Gittings, Chris Postons, Gerald Bourne, Brian Apperley, ...,............ Joe Apperley, Rodney Evans, Peter Reynolds, Graham Evans, Stephen Reynolds.

Orleton School 1955

Back Row:- L to R ...., David Wall, Lionel Edwards, ..., Dave Lewis,
Leslie Bufton, Gary Duncalfe, Mike Sheppard, ..., Eddie Lewis, Douglas Lowe, John Walters, ...,
Billy Burgoyne.

Third Row:- Mrs. Price, Pearl Mantle, Anthea Lowe, Beryl Powell, Pat Carpenter, Kathy Sheppard, ..., Joan Bufton,
Pat Wright, Jean Fortey, Doris Phillips, Shirley Angell, Jean Underwood, Margaret Cooper, Margaret Gittings, Peter Brooks,
Gerald Jones.

Second Row:- Joe Apperley, Janet Jones, Jane Basham, Doreen Kennett, Carol Tranter, Margaret Tranter, Ann Carpenter,
Barbara Wall, Rosemary Underwood, Chris Phillips, Elizabeth Cork, Jennifer Burgoyne, Miss Mary Clarke.

Front Row:- ...., Francis Jones, ..., Donald Deakin, Roger Ingram, ..., Gerald
Bourne, Brian Apperley, Philip Apperley, ..., Rodney Evans, Ken Mantle.

Orleton School 1957/58

Back Row:- L to R John Walters, Gerald Bourne, Francis Jones, David Bufton, Roger Ingram, Richard Ball,
Gerald Angell, Clive Everall, Philip Apperley, Rodney Evans, Peter Morris, Eddie Lewis, Donald Deakin.

Third Row:- Michael Wright, Joe Apperley, Shirley Angell, Jennifer Burgoyne, Rosemary Underwood, Christine Phillips,
Margaret Gittings, Pat Edwards, Janet Jones, Margaret Evans, Roger Everall.

Second Row:- Robert Lewis, Michael Lewis, ..., Margaret Tranter, Carol Tranter,
Linda Ingram, Janet Gittings, Ann James, Cheryl Duncalfe, Janet Ingram, Julie Duncalfe, ...,
Daphne Apperley, Liz Williams, Ken Mantle.

Front Row:- Peter Reynolds, Norman Evans, Steven Reynolds, Edward James, Graham Evans, Martin Jones,
David Bradbury.

Orleton School 1960

Back Row:- L to R:- Mrs. Price, Clive Everall, Gerald Bourne, David Bufton, Francis Jones, ..., ..., Rodney Evans, Philip Apperley, Peter Morris, Miss Jennifer Lewis.

Third Row:- Janet Ingram, ..., ..., Cheryl Duncalfe, - Higgins, Anne Higgins, Rosemary Underwood, Janet Jones, Margaret Gittings, Chris Phillips, Pat Edwards, Janet Gittings.

Second Row:- Roger Ingram, Linda Postons, Imelda Evans, ..., ..., Julie Duncalfe, ..., ..., Linda Ingram, ... Tranter? .... Tranter? Daphne Apperley, Peter Reynolds, Joe Apperley.

Front Row:- ...., ..., ..., Michael Lewis, Martin Jones, David Bradbury, ..., ..., Norman Evans, John Underwood, David Ingram, Gerald Angell, Robert Lewis, Richard Ball.

69

1965.

Before the present Orleton School was built the pupils had to have their games either on the field below the Old School (known as the Bottom Field) or by kind permission of the Apperleys on Pitch Block, (the field next to the Church yard which extends down to Tunnel Lane).

This photograph shows a cricket game on the Bottom Field. Les George is the wicket keeper; John Williams has his hand on his hip. Clive Anson and John Underwood can also be recognised.

Practising for Sports Day 1960's?

The sack race preparation on Pitch Block. Mr. Geoff Butcher the Headmaster can be seen left middle in the distance. This field was kindly loaned by the Apperley family for sports events and other occasions in the days before the school had a playing field.

Orleton Primary

Shropshire Journal
November 11th 1971
Pictures of Orleton School pupils. Can you find yourself?

Orleton Primary

Shropshire Journal
November 11th 1971
Pictures of Orleton School pupils. Can you find yourself?

Shropshire Journal November 19th 1971

Your School

A tank of water in the grounds of Orleton's Voluntary Aided Junior and Infants School is a success symbol. Not particularly because the school has a learner's swimming pool, but because parents of three villages could work together to buy it.

And the story of co-operation does not finish there - parents took just over a year to raise £900 to pay for the pool and a water heater - now they are working to pay for a roof over the pool and the installation of heating equipment. So far they have raised £1,200.

When the last penny is raised, parents and friends will be able to sit back and watch someone else raise the roof. They cleared the site of the pool, and erected it themselves.

The solidarity of purpose came into being when the new school was built and opened in January, 1968 at a cost of £40,000. It replaced Orleton's mid-19th century building and took children from Brimfield and Little Hereford.

The child population of the village is increasing as more and more houses are built, but the amalgamation of the three schools gave the Orleton school its biggest boost.

When the children from Brimfield and Little Hereford came to the school in April 1968, headmaster Mr. Geoffrey Butcher and his staff had 143 pupils. Today this number is down to 137, but it has been as high as 160, making the addition of the present moveable extension necessary.

Mr. Butcher saw the school through its transition period and feels of everything that happened; a meeting called by P. E. organiser Mr. Miller in October 1968, was the most crucial.

From this came the effort and enthusiasm needed to raise money for the swimming pool. A committee was formed and started on a round of fetes, coffee mornings, whist drives and other fund raising activities.

"It was an excellent committee and it had wonderful help from parents, managers, staff and the children themselves. The pool project has been a good way of bringing the parents of the three villages together to work and meet socially, in the interests of their children and the school. We hope that eventually that every child leaving this school will be a swimmer," said Mr. Butcher.

Orleton school is one where the three R's, combined with the best of modern teaching methods, are still given their traditional importance in the curriculum which aims at preparing children to go on to the Wigmore Comprehensive School.

"We aim to give a broad education. We believe the three R's, writing, reading and arithmetic, are still a basic requirement of each child," says Mr. Butcher.

Out of school hours he runs the village youth club, which draws children from the school and surrounding villages.

Several of the school's violinists have been accepted for the Herefordshire County Youth Orchestras. "We have two extremely good music teachers - Mrs. G. Woolley, violins and Mrs. D. Pembury, general music," he said. Fond of music himself, Mr. Butcher finds there is a lot of music in children. "We put on concerts and a carol service and we like to visit the other villages, Brimfield and Little Hereford. We go to one or other of these two places to give a carol service at Christmas and in this way the children from those villages can still contribute something to their community," he said.

"Before the amalgamation of the three schools there were some protests from those who did not want to lose their own schools. Since the new building has been opened it has been a unifying influence among the three villages."

Orleton School 1967-68
Mr. Geoff Butcher, Headmaster can be seen nursing a pupil.

Orleton School Staff 1970s
L to R Back Row:- Miss James, Miss Pam Sparey, Mrs. Edwards, Mrs. Wall, Mrs. S. Sparey.
Front Row:- Mr. Walters, Mr. G. Butcher (Head), Mrs. Rowe.

Orleton School Staff 1970s
L to R Back Row:- Ann Tatlow, Mrs. S. Sparey, Mrs. Wall, Mrs. A. Butcher, Mrs. S. Plant.
Front Row:- Miss D. Owens, Mr. G. Butcher, Miss James.

Orleton School Swimming Pool Committee
January 1971
L to R standing:- Mr. G. Butcher (Headmaster), Mrs. F. Apperley, Mrs. E. Sparey, Mr. C. Harris, Mr. B. Davies.
Sitting:- Mr. J. Perrott, Mrs. J. Corfield, Mrs. P. Powell, Mrs. A. Eckley, Mr. J. Layton.
"The Committee organised a very successful dinner and dance which took place at the Swan Hotel Tenbury Wells. Over 180 people attended and a profit of just over £70 was raised."

(Ludlow Advertiser 1971):- "With £900 raised in a year against their target of £2000 for a swimming pool at Orleton V.C. School, the pool fund committee last week organised a dinner and dance. It was hoped that the evening would result in a further £50 towards the Fund."
Photograph from L to R:- Mrs. Gill Perrott, Mr. Colin Finch, Mrs. Gill Finch, Mr. Fred Apperley, Mrs. Margaret Sparey, Mr. Michael Perrott.

New School Extension 1980s

At the time when Miss Daphne Owens was Headteacher the school became desperate for space. A self help scheme developed and this group of well known local fellows with others helped build a much needed extension.

L to R:- Patrick Faulkner, Joe Apperley, Frank Hulse, Peter Plant, Michael Sparey, Michael Crofts.

Orleton School Production Early 1980s
Sweeny Todd the Barber

Group includes:- Robert Bourne, Maria Stinton, Trina Ellis, Kate Plant, Karen Jenkins, Jane Apperley, Karen Bourne, Marie Yelland, Sarah Smith, Duncan Brookes, Clare Brookes, Nick Turner, Neil McClean, Alison Hamer, Jill Francis, Carla Sheppard, Collete Brown, Richard Bufton, Robert Shears, Natasha Jones.

Orleton School Staff 1980s
L to R Back Row:- Mary James, Mrs. Wall, Ann Harris, Ann Jenkins,
Front Row:- Geoff Yates (Dep. Head), Daphne Owens (Headteacher), Nan Griffiths.

Orleton School Staff 1987
L to R:- Ann Jenkins, Ann Harris, Geoff Yates (Acting Head), Jenny Hughes, Nan Griffiths.

Y.F.C.

Orleton YFC 1964
Chairman Gordon Morris attends a National Basketry Proficiency presentation by the County Chairman.
L to R:- Gordon Morris, Josephine Morgan, County Chairman, Margaret Watkins, Ann Edwards. Ann became the first lady chairman of the Club in 1963.

An important Y.F.C. occasion in the Village Hall in 1965.
Pictured from left to right are Clive Harris, Mary Harris, Mrs. Homfray-Cooper, Canadian visitor Jim Moore, John Crofts, Beryl Crofts, Gordon Morris and Mrs. Moore.

Orleton Y.F.C. Re-union 1976

A special re-union party was held by Orleton Young Farmers Club at Cawley Hall Eye. More than 130 past and present members attended. The Club's first President returned from Canada after 34 years to attend the dinner.

Pictured left to right are Mrs. H. Beaumont, the President's wife, Mr. Derek Parkes the first President, Mrs. Homfray-Cooper, Mr. John Williams Club Chairman, Mrs. Parkes, Mr. Homfray-Cooper, Mr. Henry Beaumont President. Mrs. Homfray-Cooper was the Herefordshire county organiser at the time of the Club's foundation in 1943.

John Crofts

John lived with his parents at Holmleigh (Bower Orchard, Church Lane). When he married Beryl they made their home at Hewell Cottage.

He was known far and wide as an antique specialist with Russell, Baldwin and Bright and everyone who came into contact with him admired his expertise.

He was an excellent host. If he took you to an event he introduced you to everyone with whom he came into contact. He never left you unattended. No matter where you met or what the occasion John would know you. Everyone was treated by him with interest and courtesy and made to feel of worth.

John encouraged and inspired many young people especially members of Orleton Young Farmers' Club. He always recorded results at Rallies and other competitions, congratulated those who did well, commiserated with those who didn't and commended them for having had the courage to enter. He was Chairman of the Club in 1949, Leader in 1950 and President in 1955 and 1967.

He was Clerk of Orleton Parish Council for many years.

He loved fun and provided fun for others too.

Everyone who knew John has special, individual memories of this special person. One of our many memories was of him as Father Christmas. In the 1960s we were feathering Christmas turkeys at Portway. The children were told that Father Christmas was going to make a visit.

As lunch time approached someone rushed round the corner and said Father Christmas had been shot outside Leominster. Children's mouths dropped open in disbelief. However some wise mum said, "Don't take any notice children, it's impossible to shoot Father Christmas, he'll be here soon." Sure enough as the snow began to gently fall Father Christmas came round the buildings on his dinky tractor, ringing his big, brass bell and pulling a sledge bulging with presents.

It was a sight to remember. John almost convinced the adults he was indeed the real Father Christmas.

Orleton Y. F. C. 1976

The Club has a tradition of helping senior citizens in the locality. Here young farmers can be seen delivering logs given by Mr. Reg Grosvenor of Comberton, to Mr. & Mrs. Arthur Moyle.

L - R:- Andrew Williams, Geoff Crofts, Roger Williams and Kevin Conod.

Orleton Y.F.C. 1974
With the help of County Chairman Tony Davis, Roger Williams and Kevin Conod remove an old hedge.

1981 Desert Island Risks
Orleton Y.F.C. entry came 2nd in Orleton Village Fete parade, which started from the Boot Inn.
L to R Back Row:- Helen Jenkins, Kate Sparey, Ann Powell, ..., Carol Heather, Catherine Fletcher, ..., Richard Jones, ..., Sarah Turner, Carol Sparey.
Front Row:- Trina Sparey, Wendy Wozencroft, Clare Morgan.

Orleton Y.F.C. 1982

Orleton Y.F.C. held an entertainment evening at the Village Hall and combined it with a wine and cheese party. Money raised was for church funds. The Vicar, Rev. J. T. Vivian Jones is being introduced to four of the players by Mr. Barry Francis, entertainment producer. The players are Helen Jenkins, Tim Murray, Adrian Jones and Robin Plant. The entertainment was a Fairy Tale Supertime - nursery rhymes with added humour.

Orleton Club has had a tremendous success record in entertainment and drama competitions, having won the West Midlands Finals on a number of occasions and reached the Southern Area Finals at Weymouth. This has been due in no small part to the tremendous enthusiasm, commitment, flair and talent of Barry Francis, Orleton's Producer for many years. Sadly Barry died prematurely at the age of 50 in December 1995.

It is impossible to gauge how much the Y.F.C. movement gained from being blessed with the life of this man. But! generations of youngsters undoubtedly owe him an enormous debt. As a result of his encouragement they are equipped with confidence and a sense of fun which will be invaluable to them in future years. Thank you Barry!

Fairytale Supertime 1982

Rev. J. T. V. Jones talking to Y.F.C. cast Tim Murray, Trina Sparey. ...., Clare Morgan, Adrian Sparey, Barry Francis (producer).

Middle Row:- Adrian Jones, ..., Helen Jenkins, Carol Sparey, Jill Sparey, Steve Woodfield, Catherine Fletcher, Wendy Wozencroft, Dot Connop (Choreographer).

Front Row:- Paul Morgan, ..., Phil Woodfield, Pam Rees, Audrey Bertinat, Robin Plant, Clare Brooks, Henry Faulkner.

Orleton Y.F.C. Rally 1988

L to R:- Carol Fox, Richard Fox, Clare Morgan, Neil Postons, Glenn Jones, Catherine Fletcher, Wendy Wozencroft.

The Annual Rally is a very important event in the Y.F.C. calendar. All 19 Herefordshire clubs meet at a suitable venue and compete in a wide range of events, such as football, tug-of-war, cake icing, demonstrations of skills and exhibits of work.

County Rally 1988, when Karen Jenkins, Jill Francis and Debbie Cox helped Orleton Club win the cup for gaining the most points by members under the age of 18 years.

Glenn Jones with his exhibit at the 1988 County Rally. Orleton Club was very proud of Glenn when in 1994
he became National Chairman.

Preparing a Y.F.C. exhibit at Portway Farm.
L to R:- Karen Jenkins, Sarah Smith, Gail Algar, Adrian Sparey, Patrick Baxter.

Churchyard Mowing 1988
L to R:- Phil. Woodfield, Sarah Walter, Rev. Peter Walter, Adrian Jones, Steve Woodfield, Carol Sparey, Helen Jenkins,
Catherine Fletcher, Mark Conod, Alistair Lewis, Neil Postons.
Front:- Karen Jenkins, Jill Francis.

Goings on in the Glade 1988 Rafferty's Motor Car.
L to R:- Paul Creswell, Alistair Lewis, Neil Pritchard, Henry Faulkner, Ian Godding.

"That was good Gladys" 1990 Produced by Barry Francis

Back Row L to R:- Steve Woodfield, Andrew Barker, Adrian Sparey, Mark Jones.

Next Row:- Luke Conod, Becky Rowley, Lara Conod, Jonathan Crofts, Bev. Treacy, Graham Jenkins, Alistair Lewis, Ian Godding, Richie Freeman.

Next Row:- Glenn Jones, Sarah Walter, Kathy Godding, Jill Francis, Debbie Cox, Sue Jones, Karen Jenkins, Sarah Cox, Pam Rees.

Front Row:- Samantha Pearce, Stephanie Owen, Sara Jane Crofts, Lindsey Freeman, Hazel Hulse, Gill Atherley, Sarah Smith.

Car washing frolics (Late 1980s). Glenn Jones, Adrian Sparey and Mark Conod putting more energy into soaking each other than the cars.

Baking cakes for charity fund raising 1990.
L to R:- Sarah Walter, Annette Hughes, Mark Jones, Alistair Lewis.

Orleton Y.F.C. Production
Goings on in the Glade 1980s
Back L to R:- Alistair Lewis, Steve Woodfield, Ian Godding.
Middle:- Lucinda Lloyd, ..., Robina Lloyd, Jonathan Crofts, Carol Sparey, Luke Conod, Debbie Pritchard, ..., Pam Rees.
Front:- Jill Francis, Jane Strutt, Karen Jenkins, Natasha Jones, Sarah Walter.

National Finals of Crop Management Competition 1990
Graham Jenkins being presented with his award as a member of the winning Herefordshire team.

A happy group of Young Farmers at the wedding of Graham and Bev. Jenkins. Outside St. George's Church, August 8th 1991.

Orleton Y.F.C. holding a Ploughing Marathon by kind permission of Mr. George Lewis on his land in 1991 to raise funds for the county.

L to R:- Mr. Graham Jenkins (Chairman and organiser) Mr. Ade Jones (President), Mr. Jim Apperley, Mr. George Lewis, Mr. Adrian Sparey.

Cubs
and
Brownies

Ashford, Richards Castle and Orleton Annual Cub Camp, Ashley Moor Farm 1974

Mums and Dads were invited along to the closing ceremony which included songs around the bonfire and presentation of awards for best bivouac.

Photo includes:
Back L to R:- Adrian Sparey, Neil Postons, Jonathon Webb, Adrian West, Paul Robert-Shaw.
Middle:- Roger Francis, Mr. Broome, Mrs. Johnson, Scarlet Feather, Mr. Johnson, Graham Jenkins, Hugh Morris.
Front:- Kyle Glestone, Roger Froggatt, Nick Goodwin, Robert Davies, Stephen Froggat

Cubs   Mr. Eric Broome of Richards Castle

For years this postman organised cubs for Orleton and Richards Castle. He held regular meetings at Richards Castle Club Hut.

All cubs had a tremendous affection and respect for Eric. He was an exceptional man, someone very special who should never be forgotten by Orleton Community.

He told that while a boy during World War II he was evacuated to this area. Orleton people made him very welcome and for this reason he was very grateful and developed a binding relationship. As a result it was his wish that when he grew up he would try to give something back to Richards Castle and Orleton. Through cubs he did this a hundred fold.

There is no cub I am sure who cannot recall travelling 'the great distance to Ashley Moor for a week-end camp, building bivouacs and camp fires.' Boys had such great faith in this man, so much so that whatever assignment he gave them they would earnestly attempt.

Ann and I remember going to Church Stretton to support a cub swimming gala. Our son Graham was entered for the dive event at the deep end. He came to his mum and told her what he had to do. She said "But you can't dive." Graham's reply was, "But I must do it for Mr. Broome." So there we were watching our little lad diving in and wondering whether he would surface or need to be fished out. All was well. Nothing seemed impossible with Eric's encouragement.

Orleton Cubs, Ashley Moor Camp
Photograph includes:- Back L to R: Mr. Eric Broome, helpers and Mr. Broome's son.
Second Row:- Adrian Sparey, Adrian West, Neil Postons, Nick Goodwin, Graham Jenkins,
Ali Lewis, Stephen Froggat, Robin Tibbles
Front Row:- Greville Lewis, Andrew Harris, Roger Froggat, Robert Brown, Paul Robertshaw

Mr. Dennis Aldridge of Hewell, Chairman of Orleton Parish Council planting the first tree at the New Village Hall (Early 1970s) with the help of the Brownies.

Mrs. Mary Williams (Brown Owl) is right at the back, almost hidden.

The group includes, Marg Bowen, Wendy Cade, Leslie Fortey, Suzanne Wall, Janice Butcher, Ann Bradbury, Gaynor Butcher, Susan Apperley, Kay Griffiths, Janice Vaughan, Sally Grosvenor, Sian Evans, Helen Harris.

Orleton Brownies 1970s, Tree planting Ceremony at the Village Hall.
Back L to R:- Mrs. Aldridge, Mrs. Vaughan, Edie Radnor, Ena Sparey.
Third Row:- Mrs. Yates, Mrs. Mary Williams (Brown Owl), Janice Butcher, Monica Martin,——, ——, Sarah Yeoward.
Second Row:- Pam Vaughan, Hilary Butcher, Wendy Cade, Marg Bowen, Leslie Fortey, Ann Bradbury, Sue Apperley, Janice Vaughan, Kay Griffiths.
Front:- Suzanne Wall, Gaynor Butcher.

Orleton Cubs 1940s

Photo includes:- *Front:*- John Brooks, Nigel Fuller, David Lewis, Terry Smith, Michael Cork, John Lewis.
Second Row:- John Basham, Raymond Duggan, Peter Price.
Back:- Mr. Basham, Mr. Bryant.

Orleton Youth Club

Organised by Mr. George Millichamp who lived at The Stores, Eagle House. This photograph was taken in the Old Parish Room at the Christmas party in 1950. Mr. Butcher, head teacher of the village school later led the Club. Many past members will recall how much time he put in for young people even taking them on excursions to Europe.

Back Row L to R:- Michael Heapey, Shiela Brinkley, Ivy Thomas, Roger Sparey, Michael Ball, Les Lines, Cath Collings, Anthea Bennett.
Third Row:- Pauline Jones, ————, John Brooks, Alan Wall, Norah Lewis, Audrey Powles
Second Row:- Janet Brinkley, Cynthia Brinkley, Terry Smith, Christine Jones, Jean Fortey, Lionel Edwards, Gary Duncalfe, Peter Brooks, Joan Collings.
Front Row:- Nigel Brinkley, Neil Brinkley, Derek Fortey, Michael Sparey, John Duggan, Dennis Edwards.

Sports
Teams

Orleton Football Team 1923 - 24

Back Row L to R:- Mr. Powis (Green Lane) George S. Price (Claremont), Jim Gale (Butcher's shop behind The Boot), Ray Holt (The Forge), Harry Passey (Tunnel Lane), Harry Postons (Ye Olde House), Tom Dyer (Green Lane), Mr. Webb (The Boot Inn).

Front Row:- Tom Powis (Jnr), Jack Griffiths (Comberton), Jack Williams (next to Claremont), Harry Sheppard (Comberton), George Handley (The Bower/Woodside).

Orleton Football Team 1926 - 27

Back Row L to R:- Mr. Williams, Jack Holt, Mr. Cleeton, Jack Collings.
Third Row:- Mr. Webb, Jack Griffiths, J. Gale, C. Bounds, B Bounds, T. Dyer
Second Row:- T. Powis, H. Passey, J. Roberts, J. Williams, G. Handley.
Front:- S. Passey, J. Abberley.
Victor Lewis is on the extreme right. He was a well known cricketer in the area. There must have been a match on that particular day because he is dressed in his whites.

Orleton School Football Team. 1930/31

Mr. Barrow was the Headteacher's husband. As a result of 'gasing' he was pensioned from the First World War and he used to help the boys with football.
Back L to R:- Tom Davies, Jim Ingram, Stan Grosvenor
Middle:- Dave Williams, Wilf Matthews, Sid Lloyd
Front:- Wilf Vaughan, Jack Sparey, Roland Bradford, Tom Hill, Douglas Bradford
In those days the lane between Heapey's Bakery and the Old School was very wide and Mr. Barrow drove his car down it regularly to park it in a garage which was situated on the school playground.

Woofferton Football Team 1937 - 1938
Back L to R includes:- F. Chadd, J. Cooper, T. Wright, K. Edwards, J. Jones, C. Parker.
H. Mantle, W. Sparey, - Preece.
P. Law, T. Nottingham, T. Chadd (Capt), M. Samuels, H. Thomas.
This was for the North Herefordshire League Challenge Cup, and Sir Robert Gerem-Price Sportsmans' Cup.

Pick of the League Cricket Team 1950
Back Row L to R:- Vince Tudge, —, —, —, Bill Sparey, Maurice Carpenter.
Front:- Ray Fortey, —, Dennis Postons, Geoff Smith, Alan Scriven

Orleton scores a Century in Pound notes Newspaper report 1950s

"For the second time in under three months the people of Orleton have raised over £100 for a worthy cause. Last Thursday at a dance and competition organised by Mr. G. H. Millichamp for the benefit of Ray Fortey, the sum of £136-7s-2d was realised. Ray, Orleton and Brimfield CC's wicket keeper suffered permanent injury to his leg in a motor accident last Autumn and his team mates rallied round to help him.

Prizes in the extremely successful competition were given by club members. Mr. E. Evans of Ludlow, was commended for the part he played in the competition.

At the carnival dance held in the Parish Hall, nearly 200 people danced to Millichamp's music, compered by Mr. A. Marshall, Orleton's own "disc jockey". For this dance Messrs. G. Corke, D. Dipper and G. Millichamp were door stewards and the refreshments were in the hands of Mrs. Price, Mrs. Powles, Mrs. Fortey."

Orleton Cricket Team 1956, when they beat Eyton in the local Knock-Out-Cup
Back Row L to R:- Michael Sparey, Mick Cadwallader, John Evans, Desmond Fortey, Michael Ball, Dick Tipton (Village Policeman).
Front Row:- Alan Wall, Roy Gittings, Jim Collings, George Morgan, John Lewis.

Cricket was played on the field opposite Portway Farm which belonged to Mr. J. M. Sparey. The photograph was taken in front of the 'Pavilion'. This sheet iron construction was brought on a lorry by Mr. Jim Collings from Wolverhampton where it had been made for the team by Mr. Cyril Sparrow in 1947. Cyril was a steel erector and contractor who used to come to Orleton to see the Scriven family. He would be interested to know that the building was moved to the present recreation ground and is still used although it has a lovely new pavilion standing nearby.

Bowling at The Maidenhead 1940s
Centre Mr. Charles Vale *and right* Mr. Vale's son.

W. I.

Orleton W. I. 1960's

Birthday Party in the Old Village Hall

Back Row L to R:- Mrs. Tipton, Mrs. Elsie Ingram, Mrs. Margaret Williams, Mrs. Jessie Sparey.
Middle Row:- Mrs. Mary Angell, Mrs. G. Price, Miss Margaret Vaughan, Miss Mary Clarke, ———, Mrs. Rose Manning,
Mrs. Mary Lowe, Mrs. Parton, Mrs. Annie Loxton, Mrs. Winifred Morris.
Front:- Mrs. Beryl Crofts, Mrs. Mary Worthing, Mrs. Luckett, Mrs. Dyer, Mrs. Postons, Miss Moore, Mrs. Joan Edwards.

W. I. Choir 1965

Back L to R:- Miss Edie Radnor, Miss Maude Sparey, Mrs. Dorothy Griffiths, Mrs. Jean Peverett, Mrs. Kitty Stokes, Mrs. Annie Loxton, Mrs. Yates.
Front:- Mrs. Nora Marsh, Mrs. Joan Edwards, Mrs. Audrey Cade, Mrs. Mollie Bowen, Mrs. Carol Lewis, Mrs. Ann Jenkins.

1969 Orleton W. I. New Year's Party

Members of Orleton W.I. and their friends gathered last week at the New Village Hall for the Institute's annual New Year's party.

As usual a fancy dress parade was one of the highlights of the evening. Peter Emerson, John Crofts and Harry Conod came along as three comical clergy. They amused everyone by singing a ditty based on the W.I.

W. I. New Year's Party 1969
Ludlow Advertiser
The three wives of the three clerical gentlemen formed a singing trio, 'The Beverley Sisters'. L to R: Beryl Crofts, Rita Emerson, Yvonne Conod.

Geoffrey Crofts, General Assistant, with Mrs. Molly Bowen, the Producer, working on the music with Miss Maude Sparey, pianist for W. I.
Oct 1969 (Orleton Village Hall)

W. I. Party 1969
Miss Winter Sales
meets the
Stop Go Travel Agency;
Mrs. Ann Jenkins and Miss Edie
Radnor.

W. I. New Year's Party 1969

Mrs. M. Julian came along as
'I'm Backing Britain'
and Mrs. Kitty Stokes was dressed
ready to tidy up with pail,
mop, duster and polish
as 'Mrs. Mop'.

W. I. Party 1969
Who's this gorgeous creature? None other than Michael Sparey with his binder twine wig.

W. I. Party 1969

Jack and Jill and Friends.

Left to Right:- Alf Jenkins, Carol Lewis.
Middle:- Who's this? Joyce Preece.
Front:- Jill Crofts, Miss Emerson, Sylvia Sparey.

Ludlow Advertiser October 2nd 1969

The drama group of Orleton Women's Institute are in great demand again, now that the summer has drawn to an end. On Tuesday the Group put on a variety show. Different acts included, 'We're a couple of Swells', and 'Umbrella Man'.

As a climax to the show, one of the members, Mrs. Joyce Preece from Luston, received a telephone call from Pete Murray (radio and T.V. personality) on his new morning radio show, "Free House".

"We're a couple of Swells". Mrs. Joyce Preece (left) and Mrs. Carol Lewis.

Oct 1969 (Orleton Village Hall).,

Orleton W. I. October 1969. "The Mods" show a leg to the audience. Swinging high are Mrs. Beryl Crofts, Mrs. Sylvia Sparey, Mrs. Anne Postons and Mrs. Brenda Preece.

Orleton W. I. October 1969. Miss E. Radnor - the Keep-fit teacher's nightmare. She finds that a corset is just "not the thing" for a keep-fitter, so much to the amusement of her fellow keep-fit members, she unlaces and slings it away.

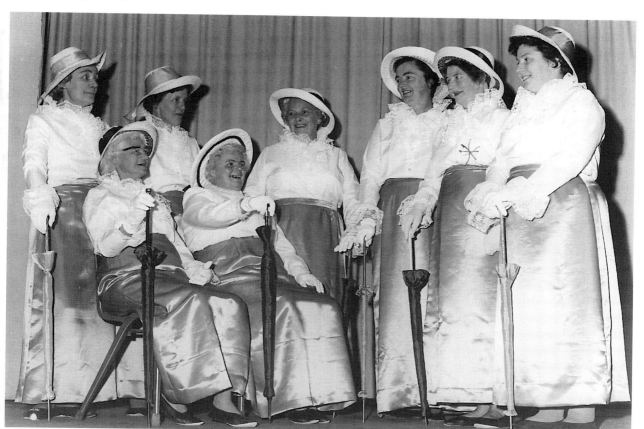

Orleton W. I. October 1969. The opening number in the Village Hall concert was performed by Mrs. A. Loxton and Miss E. Radnor *(seated) and standing left to right* Mrs. J. Edwards, Mrs. R. Worthing, Mrs. H. Smith, Mrs. M. Williams, Mrs. F. L. Yates and Mrs. O. Postons.

Ludlow Advertiser 1969/70

The report said, "A new venture for the young people of Orleton took place at the Village Hall on Saturday". It was organised by the Orleton Football Club. The evening started with some very colourful entertainment from the Gaity Girls of Yarpole and the Orleton W.I. This was followed by a family dance to the music of Dick Lea.

Back Row:- Joan Edwards, Joyce Preece, Mrs. Smith, Mollie Bowen, Margaret Williams, Mrs. Yates, Mary Worthing.
Middle:- Carol Lewis, Edie Radnor, Mrs. Loxton, Miss Maude Sparey, Mary Williams.
Front:- Olive Postons, Ann Postons, Brenda Preece, Beryl Crofts.

Mollie Bowen's Keep Fit Class 1970s
L to R:- Joan Edwards, Brenda Preece, Ann Postons, Sylvia Sparey, Mollie Bowen, Beryl Crofts, Mary Williams, Jill Crofts.

Ludlow Advertiser February 1973. Orleton W. I. Annual Dinner.

The President Mrs. Mollie Bowen welcomed about 100 guests to the Village Hall. An excellent meal was provided and a bar by the Boot Inn. Entertainment was organised by Mr. Brian Cade and Mr. Alf Jenkins with Geoff Byard providing music.

L to R:- Peter Robinson, Don Lloyd, Michael Sparey, Sylvia Sparey, Vera Lloyd, Mr. Peveritt, Jean Peveritt, Horace Percival, Mollie Bowen *(President)* Mary Worthing, Reg Worthing, Yvonne and Harry Conod in the background.

W. I. Party Village Hall 1973

L to R:- Mrs. V. Patrick, Tom Apperley, Ken Postons, Ann Postons, Olive Postons, Kitty Stokes, ———, Jean Peveritt, Phil Postons, Sybil Griffiths, Fred Apperley, Margaret Apperley, Sylvia Apperley, Ron Patrick.

W. I. Party February 1973
Mr. Reg Worthing, Mrs. Mary Worthing (Jnr), Mr. Ron Butcher, Mr. Geoff Crofts, ———, Mr. Andrew Saer,
Miss Margaret Baker, Mrs. Gladys Saer, Mrs. Connie Butcher, Mr. John Worthing.

W. I. Dinner 1973
Village Hall, back table L to R:- Idris Lewis, ———, Joe Morris, Dave Williams, ———, Bill Williams, Mrs. Wall.
Centre:- Joan Edwards, Ken Edwards, Mr. Byard, Geoff Byard, Mrs. Byard, Carol Lewis, Edie Radnor, Dave Lewis, Joyce
Preece.
Front:- ———, ———, ———.

This record shows some of the forty members and guests having their annual dinner at the Boot Inn in January 1980. Going round the table

left to right are Margaret Williams, Meg Worthing, Joan Edwards, Carol Lewis, Dave Lewis, Miss Mitchell, Ken Edwards, Sybil Griffiths and Mrs. Pritchard.

W. I. Dinner at The Boot, 18th January 1980.
Back Left to Right:- Standing Mrs. Vera Muller, Mrs. Beryl Crofts, Mr. John Patten, Mrs. Elsie Patten, Mr. John Crofts, Mrs. Millicent Godding.
Front:- Mrs. Olive Postons, Mr. Phil Postons.

Group W. I. Halloween evening at Cawley Hall, Autumn 1987.
Left to Right:- Millicent Godding, Jill Crofts, Pauline White, Mrs. Gilbert,
————, Mrs. D. Ayres, Kate Smith.

Country Life

1906. Harry Passey and hay makers at the Bower.

Using a horse drawn mower.

A sound we all used to love to hear was the click of a horse drawn mower cutting grass in early summer. This photograph shows Mr. Jack Abberley mowing at Ashley Moor in 1921.

Summer at The Lyners Farm 1920s. Mr. and Mrs. Ern Morris (newly married). Standing at the back Barbara Wickstead, sitting with hat on, Arthur Wickstead and a relative.

1920s, Corner of Wood House. Six horses and two men 'tushing' timber.

Mrs. Bubb's farmyard (Cullis Croft). Mrs. Wickstead dares to stroke the pig watched by an aunt and uncle of young Arthur and Barbara Wickstead. 1920s.

Goggin 1920s:- Mr. Wickstead (3rd from left) has an early morning poaching lesson.

1922. Cullis Croft. Mr. Jack Davies at the front of the horse, has just brought "wealthy" visitors from Church Stretton (Sitting in the trap - note the parasol), to visit the Bubb family.

1922. Jack Davies holds the horse at Cullis Lodge while the Wickstead children and friend have a ride.

1923. The Bubb family and friends going from Orleton to Ludlow in the pony and trap.

Lyners Farm 1923. Mr. Ern Morris towards the right with trilby hat. Barbara Wickstead sitting on the gate holding a kitten. The party are enjoying watching the poultry. Arthur Wickstead sitting on the wall is being amused by Ern pretending to kiss Mrs. Bubb.

1922. Mr. Ern Morris at Lyners Farm shows Arthur and Barbara Wickstead how to feed the calves.

`Sid Edwards in Colonel Hill's cherry orchard (Manor Estate) in the 1920s.

Cherry Picking.

Colonel Hill of the Manor had very large cherry orchards. Full standard cherry trees like the one in the photograph were a common sight. My father made many fruit picking ladders similar to the one seen in use. They often had thirty rungs or more and needed props to help stabilise them. The feet of George Griffiths can be seen right at the top of the picture. He is obviously standing on a branch.

When cherries were ripe, birds were continual pests and unless checked would destroy a crop. Labourers had to resort to sleeping in sheds in the orchards. Strings attached to the trees and laden with cans were connected to each shed. Periodically as dawn approached the occupants would pull the strings and rattle the cans. This disturbed the birds for a short while but they soon returned.

Ashley Moor Carthorse in gear 1924

The Williams family. Arthur Williams (David and Bill's father). In his arms is Morgan Williams. On the shaft
L to R:- Bill Williams, Dave Williams, Winnie and Naomi Williams. The name of the carthorse was Charmer.

Ashley Moor's first Van 1945

Mr. Bill Williams is standing by a Commer van purchased from Shobdon in 1945. The photo was taken at Ashley Moor by the Farm House.

Late 1930s haymaking at Marsh Hall (Tunnel Lane). Standing on the haycart are Mr. Lew Evans and Mr. Bill Ingram. In the foreground are Mr. Tom Hill and his son Arthur who lived at Marsh Hall Cottages.

Regularly this waggon journeyed down to Woofferton Junction and collected 8 tons of coal. This was split between Marsh Hall and Mr. Weaver at Hewell House. By supplying their own transport they paid £4 for 8 tons.

Beryl Morris (Crofts) and sister Millicent (Godding) helping with the hay at their home, The Lyners (1940s).

Having a rest while binding corn at Comberton in 1940s. Left to right:- Brummidgum Bill, Mr. F. Hodges, Reg Grosvenor, and 2 more visitors from Birmingham.

Spring and lambing time are synonymous. It has always been a particular pleasure to watch groups of lambs chasing each other and playing, 'I'm the king of the castle'. A shepherd's tender care given to ewes and lambs is very special and has to be observed to be appreciated. Here Mr. Ern Morris of Lyners Farm Orleton tends his flock. Note the rick of loose hay in the background.

Stringing a hop yard on stilts.

Boys having a free ride by holding onto the thriples of a hay wagon.

Mr. F. Hodges mowing grass at Comberton in the 1940s.

Mrs. Shepherd-Munn rented rooms at Orleton House after her husband the Rev. Shepherd-Munn, vicar of Orleton, died. Miss Munn their daughter was a Sister at Birmingham General Hospital. Most weekends she came to Woofferton junction. Here we see Charlie Ingram (late of Upper House) arriving at Orleton House with Miss Munn.

Mr. Ern Morris of the Lyners using a yolk to help him carry two buckets of water. Having to carry every drop to stock was a time consuming, daily requirement. Each bucketful for the house was used with great care. Around every home there were numerous 'soft water tanks' catching the proceeds from every shower and storm. The same water was often used for washing clothes, bathing, washing hair and floors before finally watering plants. Nowadays we blithely use thirty to forty gallons in a dishwasher.

Muck Spreading

Before the days of automatic spreaders, manure was lugged out on to the fields in Spring by horse and cart and placed in evenly spaced tumps. These had to be spread by using a dung fork and very hard, tiring work it was too.

Feeding poultry at Lyners 1930. Mrs. Ern Morris and child.

Mr. Ern Morris ploughing in the 1940s at The Lyners, much more arduous and slower than using a six furrow, reversible tractor drawn implement.

Mr. Hodges ploughing at the Grosvenor's Farm Comberton in the 1940s.

A fine turn-out

Shire horses and foals at the Lyners. Miss Beryl Morris (Mrs. Beryl Crofts) and Mr. Ern Morris right. Working shire horses were required for most farm jobs until the end of the 1940s. They pulled wagons and mowing machines, ploughs, chain harrows, rolls and hay rakes; magnificent creatures, bursting with muscle and power.

Silage making was unheard of and hay making was a hit and miss affair because its success depended on plenty of warm sunshine. In hilly areas the cut grass was turned with hand rakes and shaken with pikles. When sufficiently dry two or three rows were raked into one then pushed into tumps called cocks. These were then carried on poles to a barn or corner of a field where they were built into a hayrick. Everyone worked feverishly to get the crop home and dry. Farmers were always agitated if swallows swooped low over the fields. This was a sure sign of rain.

On lower land mechanical 'cock pheasants' were used to shake, aerate and turn the drying hay. Horse rakes rowed it up before it was loaded loosely onto wagons. Nothing typified the countryside more than the sweet smell of well made hay. The hay was left in ricks until required. Then stout bladed knives were used by hand to cut enough compact hay daily for the cattle feed.

The Farm Millbrook, 1936.
Ernie Poyner, the farmer who lived at The Farm, Millbrook making hay with his horse and hay-rake in the field next to Millbrook where bungalows now stand.

Until a few years ago it was a common sight to see cattle being driven through the village when being moved from field to field. Fortunately in those days, lane hedges and gates prevented the animals straying too far and the volume of traffic was less. I dread to think what damage could be caused by a herd of cattle nowadays because the semi-suburban layout of open lawns and few garden fences make properties so vulnerable.

Dave Lewis is a true countryman and his skill with sheep and training dogs is to be greatly admired. He is to me the 'one man and his dog' of Orleton. It is a splendid sight of discipline and control to see David walking at the front of the flock down a lane, his dog at the rear, signals given but not a word spoken.

The busheller measuring the hops.

Until recently Orleton had a considerable number of hop yards. Even The Farm (Millbrook Way) had oast houses. Hop picking in early Autumn was an annual ritual looked forward to by gypsies, Midlanders and locals alike. It was an opportunity for families to obtain a much needed extra bit of cash. Many pickers who came considerable distances lived in the outhouses and barns for the duration of the season.

Each family reserved a crib. They used the same one everyday and friends were invited to join them and share the proceeds. Hop yard officials regularly cut down enough vines to keep the pickers fully occupied and as the vines were stripped cribs were moved systematically up and down each hop yard avenue.

Pickers began work early in the morning while hop yards were cool and often shrouded in mist. When cribs were full 'bushellers' came with their bushel baskets to measure the picked hops. Families frequently complained that hops were crammed unnecessarily into the baskets resulting in lower than expected pay.

I always had a ravenous appetite in the hop yard but I hated the nicotine taste from the hops on my sandwiches.

The hops were taken to oast houses to be dried and pressed into large sacks called hop pockets. Finally they were transported to breweries to become an important ingredient in the manufacture of beer. You may still hear locals refer to a misty autumn day as a 'typical hop picking day'. The last hop yards of our area have now become Ashton Fruit Farm.

Hop yard scene. Families and friends stripping the vines and filling their cribs.

Cutting corn with a binder.

What a wonderful machine this was! It cut the corn, the sails knocked it onto a rotating canvas which transported the corn up between two rollers. When sufficiently compressed, tines swung over taking twine around the bundle, automatically knotting and throwing a sheaf clear of the machine. These sheaves were collected into stooks and left in the field for a few days before being stored in ricks or barns to await the threshing machine.

Corn rabbits

News travelled fast. As the last corn was being cut, neighbours, village children and men gathered with their dogs and sticks to watch for rabbits bolting. This generated terrific excitement. Corn rabbits were considered much more of a delicacy than the ordinary rabbits because of their quick, plump growth and light coloured flesh. Note the stooked sheaves in the background.

1950s Mr. Frank Saunders in the foreground with pitch fork loading sheaves of corn at Comberton.

Cider apple pickers 1930s in the Herbert's orchard (now Mr. Apperley's opposite St. George's Crescent). On the left is Miss Palfrey who lived at No. 3 The Halletts. She lived to be a hundred and when she received a telegram from the Queen in 1972, Mr. Fred Apperley and Mr. Alf Jenkins visited her to make a presentation on behalf of Orleton Parish Council.

Before the days when farmers had bulk tanks and milk quotas, they put milk into churns, took it to the nearest lane and placed it on a high stand from where it was collected by lorry and taken either to Cadbury's Factories or bottling plants. This photograph shows a regular recurring winter scene when lanes were blocked and lorries were unable to navigate them to collect milk.

Here the enterprising farmer has put his full churns in an old tin bath and geared up his horse to pull it along the lane to the main road. Tunnel Lane has been like this many times in our lifetime, certainly in 1947 and 1963.

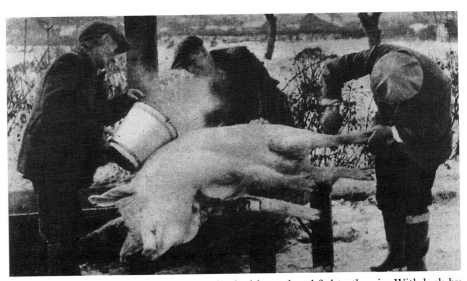

Pig killing was a sad but essential day during our childhood. Virtually every rural family kept a pig in a sty at the bottom of the garden. Domestic refrigerators and freezers were non-existent and cured bacon was a very important part of a family diet.

During spring a young pig was purchased. Household waste such as potato peelings were put into a 'pig swill' tub. Twice a day a bucketful was mixed with meal and fed to the pig. With luck by November the animal would weigh sixteen to twenty scores. However some families were unlucky enough for their pig to die and this was a real catastrophe.

Pigs were killed only when there was an 'r' in the month. At an appropriate time a furnace of boiling water was prepared, the pig was roped, heaved by half a dozen men onto a pig bench and killed by slitting its throat. Boiling water was poured over the dead pig to enable bristles to be scraped off. Clean and pink it was carried to the house and suspended from beams by its back legs with nose nearly touching the floor.

Two or three days later the carcase was cut up. Fresh joints were shared with neighbours, hams and flitches saturated with a thick layer of saltpetre for curing and sausages, scratchings and faggots made. Every part of the pig was utilised including intestines (chitterlings) and trotters. The bladder was inflated hung up to dry and used as a football.

After a few weeks in saltpetre, hams and flitches were washed clean and hung up in the house to dry. The result was bacon and ham to eat in plenty throughout the winter. A gruesome picture above people of the 90s may think, but, to country folk an essential, acceptable part of the calendar.

Chapels

Orleton Chapel and nearby Forge in the 1920s

Four Chapel stalwarts: *Left to right:*- Mrs. Jessie Sparey, Mr. Jim Sparey, Miss Maude Sparey, Mrs. Beatrice Evans. This photograph was taken in the 1980s.

Orleton Methodist Chapel

On the 3rd of December 1890 the Wesleyan Chapel was opened. An old chapel had hitherto existed on the same site, rental having been paid to the Lord of the Manor.

On the 15th August 1890 the sum of £5 was paid to the Steward of the Manor of Orleton for "costs and compensation for the sale of the land." The two names associated with the purchase of the land in 1830 were Richard Radnor (a well known family locally) and William Mason. On the opening day the sum of £166 was paid in full to Samual Evans, Builder of Orleton.

Wedding of Margaret and David Williams 1952

We are told that this was the only wedding to have been held in the Bower Chapel.

Access to the Chapel entrance is by right-of-way only as the land belongs to the owner of the 'Old Forge' adjoining. The transfer of a small piece of land giving access to the rear of the premises was negotiated with the late Jack Lewis when he lived in Chapel Terrace.

Inside the Chapel the clock was given by Mrs. Beatrice Evans and dedicated in August 1983 in memory of her late husband, Llew Evans, a life-long member and devoted Society Steward.

A furnishing fund was started, and in July 1984 carpets were bought and laid, the old pews sold and replaced by chairs.

The original pulpit was removed from its central position and a communion rail, together with a pulpit at the side was installed. These were given in memory of the late Jim Sparey and dedicated in 1988. A plaque on the pulpit records this and his years of devoted service.

The Communion Table and Chairs were Jim's gifts, made from oak grown on his farm at Portway.

His sister Maude Sparey was an inspired organist for over 20 years, until failing powers forced her to retire in 1984. 'Aunt Maude' is now 100 years old and resides at a Residential Home in Wigmore. This remarkable lady has during her life done so much to help so many people and is still known as 'Aunt Maude' to everyone. When the co-author was appointed to his first Headship he had no pianist; so 'Aunt Maude' played the Chapel organ to record every hymn in the school hymn book to enable the children to have accompaniment for assembly.

The electric organ was given to the Chapel when Peaton Chapel closed down in 1985, replacing the pedal organ.

Other enhancements over the last years have included a pulpit-fall made by Rose Maynard, a lectern, a counter and a cupboard for tea-making made by the late Bert Clarke. With his help Bill Taylor completely re-wired the Chapel and Bill recently extended the window-sills to hold flowers and harvest displays.

The late Jim Moyse converted an unrequired section of the new pulpit into the handsome cupboard at the rear of the Chapel where the new 'Hymns and Psalms' are kept.

A centenary service was held on Sunday December 2nd 1990 at 3.00pm, conducted by Rev. T. John Davies B.A. The preacher was Superintendent Minister, Rev. Brian White, and songs were sung by the Tenbury Quartet.

By Miss G. Bentley

Goggin Chapel (Orleton Common)
"The Top Chapel"

"The highlight of the year was the annual outing, usually to the sea, but, to qualify for this you had to do a party piece at the Anniversary. That meant either singing or reciting on your own and many junior members found this very hard even though it may have meant only reading a few verses from the Bible.

A platform was put up for this special day and we all felt very important as we climbed up to our seats. One of our regular adult readers had a very cultured voice and my one brother embarrassed us terribly by mimicking her while reading his few lines. When I got home I would say how naughty he had been and plead for him not to be allowed to go again.

We were only a handful of pupils and it was a long walk from Portway for a 2.30 pm start. Nevertheless we always seemed to arrive before the teacher did and so we often walked right up to Orleton Common to meet her. At other times we played in the brook while waiting getting ourselves soaking wet. This was not a sensible thing to do because the Chapel had no heating.

One of our teachers played the organ and insisted on us singing plenty of repeated choruses. Small wonder that we were always very tired by the time we had walked back home.

(Joan Edwards)

Waterloo Chapel - Goggin (locally known as The Top Chapel, 1996).

Waterloo Chapel - Goggin (1996). Built in 1848.

Orleton Church during the Second World War period.

Church

The church supposed to have been dedicated to St. George is mainly a 12th century building of local sand-stone rubble with sandstone dressings. It consists of chancel, nave, north porch, organ bay, vestry and western tower with a chamfered spire covered with oak shingles.

The church was thoroughly restored and the chancel rebuilt in 1863 -64 at a cost of about £1200 under the direction of Mr. Drew, architect of Stoney's Gate, Westminster, London. Skeletons of a large size were found under the floor and on the west wall some paintings of scripture scenes and decorative work were met with, which could not however be preserved.

"The living is a vicarage, net yearly value £192, including 84 acres of glebe, with residence, in the gift of the governors of Lucton School, and held since 1901 by the Revd. Joseph Shepherd-Munn." (Kelly's 1913).

The nave has two 14th century windows which contain fragments of old stained glass. Standing in the middle of the nave looking towards the tower a 13th century arch can be seen and above it a 12th century window arch which was in place before the tower was built.

The south wall contains two 14th century windows. The one nearer the tower contains stained glass in memory of Arthur Keysall Yapp, "whose forceful personality made the Red Triangle of the Y.M.C.A. one of the most effective moral factors at home and abroad during the 1st World War. Sir Arthur, born in Orleton, was secretary of the Y.M.C.A. when the war began and he instantly appealed for £25,000 for carrying on the work among the troops. Before the war had ended he had raised nearly £3,000,000. He introduced the Red Triangle as a symbol of the Y.M.C.A. and the value of its work can never be measured. It is only one of its hundred services to the nation that it gave a thousand million sheets of Red Triangle note-paper to our men for writing letters home. In knighting Sir Arthur Yapp, King George V declared that Sir Arthur had placed the whole Empire in his debt. In the midst of the war he handed over the Red Triangle work to a colleague and became Director of Food Economy. He had started life as a farmer's son, began preaching in chapels as a boy of 15 and joined the Y.M.C.A. at 21. He was with it for nearly half a century and no man better served his county or his country." The author had cause to stay in many Y.M.C.A.s during his forces life and therefore has a special respect for Sir Arthur.

The chancel was rebuilt in 1340. On either side of the arch are two large carved heads, the original supports of the rood beam. It is thought the large head on the North wall is that of King Edward II (1307 - 1327) with that of his Queen, Isabella, on the opposite side, facing him. Above his head is a smaller representation of Piers Gaveston, the murdered favourite of the King, whilst the mitred head on the North Side of the chancel arch is that of the Abbott of Wigmore, a King's supporter.

On the Queen's side of the arch is the head of Adam of Orleton. He was born in Orleton in 1285 and was probably baptised at the font. He became Bishop of Hereford, then Worcester and Winchester. This powerful man was a conspirator against Edward II, helped force him to abdicate and connived his assassination. Adam became blind in his latter years and died in seclusion at the age of 60, in Farnham.

At the head of the arch, looking down on the others is Roger Mortimer, Lord of Wigmore and lover of the Queen who was responsible for the overthrow of the King.

The pulpit is a delicately carved Jacobean beauty. It is a wonderful example of 17th century craftsmanship. There is a crucifix above the pulpit which we are told was carved by a Belgian refugee in 1916. Apparently it was in gratitude for the hospitality given to him by Orleton people. On the north side of the arch is a brass memorial giving the names of Orleton men who gave their lives in the two World Wars.

The 12th century stone font is much talked about and interested folk travel many miles to see it. It has nine apostles standing in arching round the bowl. They are crude, ungainly but beautiful and St. Peter is identifiable by his key.

Near the chancel arch on either side are two hollowed out chests each about 800 years old. It is a sobering thought that they were made from two oak trees which were growing in Norman England.

The chancel contains brasses and a stone slab dated between 1600 and 1700 in memory of the Blount family. The east end stained glass lancet windows are a memorial to Letitia Ann Edwards wife of the Vicar, dated 1892 and the side windows are memorials to the Rev. Preb. William Edward Edwards M.A. vicar from 1853 to 1901. There is a 12th century vestry door on the south side and on the north side an organ chamber which was added in 1867.

In 1864-5 when the restoration was underway it was found necessary to take down the south wall and replace it. When the walls were stripped it was discovered that the whole church had been frescoed. Beneath these some very old paintings were discovered including Jacob watering a flock at a well - but unfortunately it was not possible to save any.

The south wall had been built without an adequate foundation, the roof weight had pushed it 22″ out of perpendicular and cracks 5″ wide were discovered under the chancel arch plaster.

When the western gallery was removed it was revealed that in 1720 some puritan church warden had drawn a figure of death 7′6″ high on the western wall. The figure held a coffin in one hand with a lid turning on knuckle-bone hinges and a spade in the other hand.

The chancel was re-opened on 24th October 1867, part of the work having been paid by a parish levy.

The tower was built in the mid 13th century in three stages and an octagonal timber chamfered spire built above. The tower contains three bells, one by John Finch 1639 and the other two by John Martin dated 1665.

The north porch built in 1686 of oak is mounted on low stone walls and its door is an ancient, heavy cross-banded one with long strap iron hinges.

The two clocks of Orleton Parish Church

(Extracts from an article written in Summer 1993)

The Old Clock Movement. The fact that this treasure is on display in the Nave and beautifully presented is entirely due to the patience, interest and time of Mr. Graham Hodgetts of Glebe House. How lucky we are that Graham came to Orleton and the authors are grateful he has enabled them to print these extracts.

"The Parish Church of Orleton has two clocks. The working clock which strikes the hours has an outside dial bearing the legend: 'VR 1887'. There is also the remains of an earlier turret clock and a painted dial which is now mounted inside the entrance porch ...... the present clock ...... was installed to commemorate Queen Victoria's Golden Jubilee.

The Old Clock. An old clock which must have been abandoned more than 100 years ago and left in one of the tower rooms, was found ...... in a rusty and filthy condition. Before making any assessment it was necessary to dismantle and clean it. ...... The top and bottom front cross members were missing and the newly forged iron straps were made to match the rest of the frame and to give stability ...... It is thought that the clock would run for 30-35 hours between windings ...... it is thought (tentatively) to belong to the first quarter of the eighteenth century.

A lozenge-shaped painted sheet copper dial, 3 feet 6 inches square with a wooden moulding surround is now mounted inside the tower porch ...... It is assumed that it was once the outside dial of the old clock. The old hour hand has been retained. There are quarter markings only between the hours and although badly weathered and barely decipherable in parts the legend reads:- E. Coleman, T. Yeates, Church Wardens, 1830.

The present clock ...... is believed to be by John Moore and Sons, Clerkenwell and to date from around 1810. It must have therefore been secondhand when supplied in 1887. ...... It runs for eight days between windings......

Jubilee Celebrations. Tuesday, June 21st 1887

In Orleton a Jubilee celebration committee met in the schoolroom on June 4th and was presided over by the vicar, the Revd. William E. Edwards. It was proposed ...... 'to celebrate the occasion with a dinner, tea, sports and bonfire, and as a fitting permanent memorial, to install a new clock in the church.'

Maybe they had seen a letter in the Leominster News a few weeks before where the merit of having a permanent commemoration of the Jubilee was advocated (in this case by the founding of a hospital in Leominster). To quote: "Surely the poor of the district would see for themselves how much more they would benefit by the public money being invested in this way, than by its going to provide them with a day's surfeiting and drunkenness, which seems a favourite project in some quarters!" Anyway, Orleton Jubilee committee decided to risk 'a day's surfeiting' as well as having a permanent memorial to mark the occasion. A collection was organised, and from this, a sum of £15 was set aside to cover the cost of dinner and tea for the village celebrations. Mr. G. Lawrence of the Boot Inn was asked to supply a cold dinner and cider at 1/6 per head.

The day began at 12 noon with a church service. Then to quote from the Leominster Times ...... "the male portion of the inhabitants over 15 years of age sat down to dinner in the orchard behind the Boot Inn." (No one questioned segregation or thought about discrimination in those days).

"The meal comprised beef and mutton, roast and boiled potatoes and bread, followed by cheese and with an unlimited supply of cider and perry. There were over 130 present." The vicar made a speech in which he remarked that many things which we looked upon as necessities were considered by the last generation as great luxuries. As an example he contrasted the lucifer match with the old flint and steel tinder box in order to illustrate the great technical progress in the last 50 years.

"At 3 o'clock in the evening a bonfire was lit on the hill (Lodge Farm) kindly granted by Mr. Yeld. There were 200 people present and rockets were let off. This part of the celebrations was under the management of Revd. Cyril Edwards (son of the vicar) and Mr. Aubrey Edwards (churchwarden). As many as 16 fires could be seen from this point.

The Revd. C. Edwards (son of the vicar) ...... was offered a secondhand clock by Smiths of Derby in June 1887 for £38 (a new one was £68). A dial (new) would cost £5 and a locally made protective case was also estimated at £5. It was decided to have the secondhand clock which was installed at the end of 1887. It is still giving good service in 1995."

The vestry was added in 1867 for a cost of £367 - 12 - 6d. Most of the money was given by Governors of Lucton School, patrons of the church.

In the churchyard there is a 14th century cross. The shaft is relatively new but poorly built. The top layer of the base however contains a lovely, quite well preserved niche.

"In AD 1431 Edward Earl of March gave land for a cemetery, on a representation that during the period quarter (1401 - 1425?) the frequent heavy flooding of the intermediate land presented his tenants in Orleton with great difficulty conveying their dead to the mother church of Eye, whereupon the Church of Orleton was made parochial and a graveyard consecrated and subsequently a larger church." (From notes found by Mr. C. Marsden, Orleton Manor).

Orleton Churchyard

The churchyard is traditionally thought to be the likely setting for the Resurrection when the Day of Judgement finally arrives. In the past many people from all over the country specifically requested burial here, with their feet facing the lower gate, in the hope that they would be able to make a quick getaway when brought back to life.

Those who have experienced it will know that Orleton's St. George's Church has a light, bright interior which is full of architectural interest and is a welcoming pleasant place to worship.

Orleton Band 1920s. Taken at St. George's Church Fete.

St. George's Church Choir 1930s

Back Row Left to Right:- Edwin Grosvenor, Charles Ingram, George Deely, John Deely, Reg Grosvenor, Ernie Ingram, Stan Grosvenor, Jim Ingram, Joe Radnor, Lewis Evans, Roy Gittings, George Millichamp, Phil Postons, Bill Ingram, Horace Percival.

Front:- Derek Gale, Mrs. Evans, Margaret Apperley, Edie Powles, Miss James, Rev. David Lewis, Mrs. Lewis, Ethel Radnor, Beattie Radnor, Edie Radnor, Arthur Postons.

Centre Front:- Peggy Passey.

This photograph was taken after the Three Choirs Festival in Hereford Cathedral. Mr. Grosvenor, back left, is proudly holding the banner which Orleton had won after defeating Llangorse. They had been the holders of this treasured prize for some time.

St. George's Choir 1930s

Back L to R:- Jack Holt, Bill Ingram, Mrs. Payne-Brown, Polly Passey, Lil Webb, Eleanor James, Kathy Passey, Alf Hughes, Harry George.
Front:- Jim Parton, Ernie Ingram, Jimmy Wall, Rev. Payne-Brown, Mollie Herbert, Bill Cleeton, Jim Collings.

Mr. Holt was the blacksmith at the Forge and he used to run a bus service to town. However if locals were unable to make the journey, Mr. Holt would do their shopping for them.

Church Outing 1950s

Back L to R:- Elsie Ingram, Mrs. Mapp, Isobel Porter, Mrs. Rose Manning.
Front:- Rosemary Underwood, Jean Underwood, Mrs. Parton, Chris Postons, Mrs. Postons.

143

Church Fete 1965. This was held on the 'Glebe Land' at the end of Church Lane. The lady on the right was Mrs. Deakin (Donald's Mum). Their home in Church Lane was half the black and white cottage (The Cottage in 1990s).

1965. Most village functions and church fetes were held on the 'Glebe Land' at the end of Church Lane. St. George's Church can be seen in the background. Does anyone recognise the members of the tug-o-war teams?

1984. The Rev. J. T. Vivian Jones retires after 33 years at Orleton. After a service in Orleton Church he received retirement gifts from parishioners and friends. Mrs. Elsie Ingram a choir member and friend of Mr. and Mrs. Jones for 33 years and Mr. Alf Jenkins, Church-warden, present cut glasses, a new pipe and tobacco to Rev. Jones as well as cheques totalling £500 to both of them.

Rev. J. T. Vivian Jones, the last vicar to live in the Old Rectory before it became a Residential Home for the Elderly. Rev. Jones was vicar of Orleton with Brim-field from 1952 until 1984.

Thursday 16th July 1987 Orleton Church (Shropshire Star).

'The refurbishment of Orleton Church was finished ahead of schedule due to the enthusiasm shown by a NACRO team.

Previously unemployed, the team has provided the Church with some major internal improvements. Supervisor Terry Chambers said a team led by Bob Butcher had completed repairs to the chancel, nave and tower with six weeks of the project still to run.

The project cost around £3,000 resulting in a substantial cash saving for the church.'

This was part of the major fundraising appeal work launched by Rev. Peter Walter. Other aspects were renovation of the organ and the installation of new central heating.

Pictured are from Left to Right:- Adrian Bates, Edward Pike, Bob Butcher (leading hand), Roddy Bolitho, William Bradley, Terry Chambers (supervisor). The Rev. Peter Walter with Churchwardens Mr. Bob Hinchliffe and Mr. Clive Harris are thanking the team for a job well done.

The Easter Parade, Orleton Village. During the ministry of Rev. Peter Walter this was a regular feature which took place alternately in Brimfield and Orleton Villages. The donkey leading was loaned each year by Mrs. Jenny Harrison.

Trip to York on Oct 11th 1986
Rev. Peter Walter strongly advocated that communities should do things together, not just to raise money but to develop cohesion and friendship. On two occasions during his ministry in Orleton and Brimfield we hired a train to York and Bath. They were splendid excursions. Even lunch was organised by the party on the train. This photo includes standing, Rev. Peter Walter, Michael Sparey and Alf Jenkins.

Autumn 1987
Victoriana Committee member, Mr. Geoffrey Crofts (left) and chairman Mr. Alf Jenkins, in front of Ye Olde Shoppe in Orleton, near Ludlow.

Villagers look back
Shropshire Star 1987. Orleton, near Ludlow, is taking a trip through time this weekend.

Victoriana celebrations in aid of the local church have put the clock back for visitors and residents alike.

An historic tour of the village - properties marked with old photographs and information - illustrate how things used to be.

Residents are also dressing the part for a series of fundraising events, including a pig roast at the recreation ground tonight.

A Victorian celebration to fundraising, 1987.

An article in the Ludlow Advertiser. 'A community which has raised £16,000 in just over twelve months for its historic church will be celebrating in style soon.

A Victorian weekend at Orleton will even have them dancing in the aisles at St. George's Church, centrepiece of the fundraising effort launched last March.

Lifesize cutouts of Victorian gentlewomen, made by Alf Jenkins and Sandy Burton, already point the way to the celebrations, which start on August 28 with a jazz evening in the church. The Zenith Hot Stompers' performance will combine traditional jazz with blues and spirituals. "I hope people won't be inhibited by their surroundings," said the Rev. Peter Walter.

The cash raised so far has paid for repairs to the roof and ceiling, redecoration, a new heating system and organ renovations. Another £8,000 will pay for other programmed work.

On August 29 a pig roast will be held at the recreation ground with dancing to the Caribbean Sunrise Steel Band.

On August 30th the tempo will be slower with a concert by the Vale of Arrow Choir in the church.

An organ recital by the Rev. Frank Rumball will close proceedings on Sunday evening. An historical tour, craft fair and flower festival are also planned.'

Water

Ford Millbrook, early this century

Millbrook House

An interesting house dating back to 1599 when the first part of this property was constructed and followed by two further additions, the one later in the 17th century and the other some 100 years later. The house is constructed of stone to the first floor level and half timbered on the first floor. Originally this property was thatched but is now tiled. An unusual feature in the living room on the North East is that the joist timbers have been constructed so that at the one end a height of seven feet is attained but slopes to six feet and nine inches at the other, a very peculiar feeling!

In the 1920's the property was "modernised" and the exterior walls were all plastered to give a stone effect which was modern for its time, also the original staircase was removed and a new one installed.

The house was acquired in the mid 1900's by the Marsh family who are still living there today.

The Ford

The ford was piped and bridged over for traffic in 1960. Prior to this a small footbridge was available for pedestrians and vehicular traffic had to pass through the water as can be seen from our photographs.

Many of you will remember Geoff Fuller who lived in Orchard Cottage, Church Lane, before it was modernised. He had a haulage business and regularly washed his lorry in the ford. When the water was high and dances were on at the village hall, Geoff Lines used to stand on the footbridge and make every youngster pay a fee in order to get to the dance at the old village hall. If they refused he made them walk through the water. During the last war the Home Guard used the ford for their dispatch riders to practise riding through.

Millbrook and Mill-Lane 1930s.

This is a beautiful view showing the walkway over the Ford. This is now part of the bridge. If you lean over the far rail the arches can still be seen.

1940s Ford footpath. Always a popular meeting place. Looking from Mill Lane - Ford House in the background.

Millbrook. A boy cycling through the ford in the 1940s.

Millbrook Ford, 1958.
Before the bridge was built at Millbrook a high, railed footpath about a yard high ran by the side of the road and over the Ford. Jim and daughter Cath Collings who lived at Chapel House can be seen standing above the arches of the old footpath. When this photograph was taken Millbrook Way was a narrow lane shrouded with damson trees.

The only properties in the lane were The Farm, Ford House, Millbrook House, Fairfield and The Cottage.

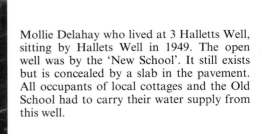

Mollie Delahay who lived at 3 Halletts Well, sitting by Hallets Well in 1949. The open well was by the 'New School'. It still exists but is concealed by a slab in the pavement. All occupants of local cottages and the Old School had to carry their water supply from this well.

From an article in January 1982 Grapevine by Mr. George Platt

"It would be unusual for any meeting of Orleton Parish Council to take place without the subject of our water supply being discussed. The November meeting was no exception - indeed even more interesting in that it was suggested, quite seriously I believe, that it might be worthwhile to revive the use of the wells that served the village before mains water was provided. To a relative newcomer, which I suppose I am, the only possibility that came to mind was Halletts Well, ... George Wall's address is Halletts. If anyone should know about the well it would be him.

Where was it, or indeed, where is it? No problem. The school has a lay-by to accommodate the children's buses. At the village end of the lay-by there is a bit of pavement and a holly tree. Under the holly tree there is an insignificant looking man-hole cover. That is Halletts Well.

George tells me that when it was in use there was a low curb of bricks surrounding the well and three steps down to a depth of water that would allow the complete immersion of a bucket ...... Where did the water come from? George tells me that when the roadway was being excavated for the installation of our sewage system, a stone culvert running into the well was exposed and in fact damaged to the extent that it was replaced with conventional brown glazed drain-pipes. However someway back towards the village the original culvert left the roadway and diverged into Church House Farm orchard. From there tradition has it that its origins were - wait for it - the church graveyard, but nobody seemed to mind that.

So much for words. Now for action. I had to see what is under the man-hole. The invaluable George produced a jemmy, and, in a minute the lid was off, and, before my very eyes was Halletts well. A plain brick chamber, no steps down, but a substantial gushing flow of pellucid water. Reverently we gazed on the spectacle. Orleton's water problem was solved. We replaced the cover and tip-toed away. It wasn't until later that I realised that I should have tasted the stuff. Perhaps another time ...... But what of the name? I had assumed that Hallett was a person, but George points out that the immediate vicinity is more properly known as The Halletts......

Local Newspaper Report, 11 Aug. 1960

'In the days of television and washing machines many villagers still have to draw and carry their water. Orleton folk are among the unlucky ones. Miss Violet Hodges (Mrs. Mollie Delahay) is seen returning to her home in pouring rain.'

154

Dickens Lane

The 'pump' in this lane was the main source of water for Church Lane prior to the mains supply being available in the early 1960s.

This snap shows Mrs. Handley carrying water in her enamel pail. Nearer the pump is a pony and trap with a milk churn, undoubtedly being filled with water. Well Cottage is shown on the left of the picture.

Dickens Lane

One of the places where the village got its water supply in the 1940s. The old pump is still there in the 1990s.

Portway Farm in the yard by the pump 1923. Mr. J. M. Sparey and Mrs. Sparey with baby and members of the Wickstead family.

1922: Mrs. Wickstead carrying water at Mrs. Bubb's (Cullis Croft).

Hereford Evening News 11th Aug. 1960: "Farmer Clive Harris has lived in Orleton for only two years, but has settled in with his family to enjoy life here. There's outside work to be done by Clive, even in heavy rain. He trims a hedge while water swirls around his boots."

This article which appeared in the Hereford Evening News on the 11 August 1960 illustrates that Orleton has always had flooding problems, but that obtaining drinking water without a mains supply was an even greater problem in those days.

"Orleton's story is, literally, one of water and beer. Water because when the brook is not flooding most of them out, the villagers ponder on employing a diviner in search of some of the stuff.

Beer, because any small village with three public houses is not unnaturally more attractive to the traveller. (The Boot, Maidenhead and The Bay Horse).

When we clapped eyes on Orleton, which stands in the shadows of nearby Woofferton Radio Station, it was in the grip of a deluge. Farmer Clive Harris of The Farm, Orleton (still named The Farm in Millbrook Way) was trimming his hedge with water swishing around his boots. Yet his chief complaint was lack of water.

'Its a curious thing that people who have such modern conveniences as television sets should have to carry water. But we do and there are only two or three wells with a decent supply,' he told me.

A little further down the road, Clive's words came home to us forcibly, for Miss Violet Hodges (Mrs. Mollie Delahay) was returning from the well, in pouring rain, with her afternoon's water supply.

Down by the Mill Brook something stirred, it was the sound of Herefordshire County Council workmen putting paid to something that has been there far too long, the ford.

The little narrow bridge, which to date has been the only way of getting across without wetting your feet, is to go. In its place is to come a 23' wide bridge, which will feature water-cuts to add ornamentation.

In the middle of the village stands the Boot, and there is a tale to be told of the original sign which dominates the front. It is appropriately enough, a huge wooden model of an old boot. Licensee, Mr. Sidney Downing, took the idea from an old door stop which he was using at the inn. He asked an artist acquaintance if he could make a sketch of it. He did so, and the job went next into the hands of a local carpenter Mr. Phil Postons.

Phil set to work in his shop and fashioned a huge replica of the old door-stop, which was then painted and hung outside the inn. The sign is now looked upon by sign experts as one of the most original in the land.

Thirty seven years old Phil Postons adopted the craft of his father as a boy. It was his father who fashioned the west doors of Leominster Priory, and many other church portals in the county are examples of his work.

Phil is something of a reminder of the days when mass production would have been frowned upon, and when craftsmen took a personal delight in a job well done.

Phil knows the craft of a wheelwright too, but there are few calls on him in that trade now. "I can't remember the last wheel I had to deal with, but it was a very long time ago," Phil told me.

He has worked in the shop at Orleton since he was 14. Phil is known in the village and many other parts of North Herefordshire, as a man who will turn down a slap-dash job, even if there is plenty of money in it."

August 11 1960. Something stirs down at Mill Brook and it isn't just the water. The old foot bridge over the ford is way out of date. The County Council are bringing the spot up to date. Workmen are just putting in one of the new "cuts" of the road bridge.

Tunnel Lane

It is often asked, "Why is it called Tunnel Lane?" In Spring and Summer it is very common to see school parties walking down the Lane to see the Tunnel.

In the 1700s it was proposed to build a canal from Kington via Leominster to Stourport. Unfortunately the unfinished canal was closed in 1859. However 18¾ miles was built between Leominster and Lindridge.

The Leominster section passed through Eye, under Tunnel Lane and through Putnal Tunnel by the side of the railway and on to Woofferton Wharf. This stretch was put to good use and in 1796 fourteen boats loaded with coal from Mamble Pits arrived at Leominster Wharf. Apparently the contents of the first boats were distributed free to the deserving poor. The remainder was sold at 15/- (75p) a ton. Prior to this the cheapest coal in Leominster was 30/- (£1.50) a ton. Clee Hill coal also found its way to the Leominster Canal.

It remained in use for 50 years but in 1852 the Hereford/Shrewsbury railway opened and the Tenbury/Kidderminster link soon followed. These lines expedited the closure of the unfinished canal. Fortunately it is still possible to see the remains of Putnal Tunnel and a short stretch of the canal running towards Eye from near Tunnel Lane.

Locals will tell you that the Tunnel Lane sign should not be at Brick Corner. Strictly speaking the stretch from the corner to the Manor junction is Rock Lane, named so because of how the original cutting had to be made. The road and 'hamlet' to Chapel Terrace is The Bower and Tunnel Lane begins at Chapel Terrace.

Putnal Tunnel 1996. From here the tunnel bores under the hill towards Woofferton and re-appears by the railway.

The only remaining stretch of Leominster Canal; looking from Putnal Tunnel towards Eye. (photo Mr. Thomas's field 1996).

Putnal Tunnel. Giving an idea of the Cutting depth. Tunnel Lane is through the trees on the skyline. (1996).

Village Hall and Fetes

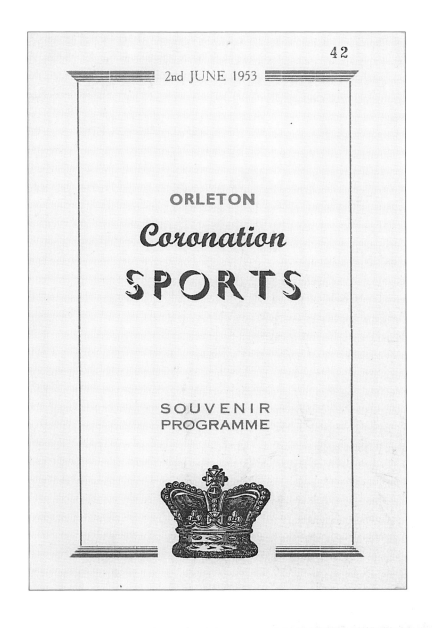

42

2nd JUNE 1953

ORLETON

Coronation

SPORTS

SOUVENIR
PROGRAMME

Orleton Coronation Sports
PROGRAMME

Event		Prizes	
		1st	2nd
1. (1.45).	SOAP BOX DERBY (Handicap)	10/-	5/-
	Route—TOWNSEND TO CHURCH *(Free Ice Cream to all Entrants)*		
2. (2.00).	PROCESSION		
	Route: ASSEMBLE CHURCH TO SPORTS FIELD, led by " MISS ORLETON."		
	FANCY DRESS:		
	Children (mixed) under 10 years	7/6	5/-
	„ „ over 10 years	7/6	5/-
	Adults (Mixed)—Comic	15/-	10/-
	„ „ Fancy	15/-	10/-
	Decorated Prams and Bicycles	15/-	10/-
	Vehicles—		
	Horse *or* Mechanical driven	15/-	10/-
	All Judging on Field		
3. (2.15).	OFFICIAL OPENING OF THE BUS SHELTER		
	by MRS. H. D. LYNES		
	for CORONATION OF QUEEN ELIZABETH II. and in Commemoration of the late KING GEORGE VI.		
4. (2.45).	TODDLERS RACE (50 yds.)		
	Five years and under—GIRLS	2/-	1/-
	„ „ BOYS	2/-	1/-
5.)3.00).	100 Yds. FOOT RACE		
	10 years and under—GIRLS (H'cap)	2/6	1/6
	BOYS „	2/6	1/6

6. (3.15).	100 Yds. FOOT RACE		
	15 years and under—GIRLS (H'cap)	2/6	2/6
	BOYS „	2/6	1/6
7. (3.30).	100 Yds. FOOT RACE		
	LADIES EGG and SPOON (H'cap)	2/6	1/6
8. (3.30).	CROSS COUNTRY CYCLE RACE	10/-	5/-
	Route: Start, Field—Ashley Moor Turn—Turn Right—Take road by Gibralter Rock—Down Rise Lane —Turn left and take road to Portway Corner (via Hungerhill). Turn Right and finish through Gate in Field where start was made.		
9. (3.45).	100 Yds. 3-LEGGED RACE		
	(Mixed), 10 and under (H'cap)	2/6	1/6
	(Mixed), 15 and under (H'cap)	2/6	1/6
10. (4.00).	OBSTACLE RACE		
	16 and over (H'cap)	5/-	2/6
11. (4.15).	COMIC FOOTBALL		
	(First Round), Six-a-side	15/-	9/-
	(Limit 8 teams). Rulings: All teams to include at least 2 ladies except Boys' teams. Association Ruling. No offside. Corners to count one point. Goals 8 points.		
12. (4.15).	RELAY RACE (4). 440 yards		
	16 and over (H'cap)	10/-	
13. (4.30).	LADIES (ONLY) CATCH THE BLACK LEGHORN COCKEREL		
	Prize —The Cockerel) (Kindly given by Mr. T. Apperley)		

14. (4.30).	220 Yards FOOT RACE		
	20 and under (Mixed)	5/-	2/6
15. (4.30).	WHEELBARROW RACE,		
	50 yards (Mixed), all ages	5/-	2/6
16. (4.45).	100 yds. FOOT RACE		
	(21—30 years) (Mixed), H'cap	5/-	2/6
	31—40 years „	5/-	2/6
17. (5.00).	POTATO & BUCKET RACE		
	(Mixed), 10 and under, H'cap	2/6	1/6
	„ 15 „ „	2/6	1/6
18. (5.15).	WALKING RACE (Heel & Toe)		
	(Mixed), 440 yds., 55 & over, H'cap	5/-	2/6
19. (5.30).	PONY AND COB RACE		
	Handicap	10/-	5/-
20. (5.30).	CART HORSE DERBY		
	Walk, Trot and Gallop	10/-	5/-
21. (5.30).	ANNOUNCEMENT OF LUCKY PROGRAMME NUMBER		
		5/-	
22. (5.45).	SLOW BICYCLE RACE		
		2/6	1/6
23. (6.00).	MUSICAL CHAIRS ON BICYCLES		
		2/6	1/6
24. (6.15).	SACK RACE (OPEN)		
		2/6	1/6
25. (6.15).	TUG-OF-WAR (Six-a-side)		
	Entries on field	15/-	
26. (6.30).	FINAL COMIC FOOTBALL MATCH.		

All winners will receive a card from the Judges and on presentation to the Treasurer (Mr. P. Sparey) they will collect their prize money immediately after Race.

Chief Ring Stewards

Mr. R. Worthing, Mr. J. Crofts, Mr. W. Lines, Mr. T. Apperley with other members of the Committee.

Football Referee - Mr. J. Angell.

Cycle Race - Mr. J. Taylor.

All Catering. Many thanks to Women's Institute members who are carrying out this very big task most efficiently.

9.0 p.m. — 2 a.m.
DANCE AND PARTY IN PARISH HALL
(Free to all Orletonians)

SIDE - SHOWS ON FIELD

SKITTLES   PILLOW POLE FIGHT

HIDDEN TREASURE — 1d. a Peg — Winner takes all.

GUESS WEIGHT OF SHEEP — 1d. a Guess — Winner takes all

BALLOON RACE: 3d. a go. Time limit for returned Labels 14 days. Prize 10/- for greatest distance.

GOD SAVE THE QUEEN

ORLETON PRINTING PRESS, LEOMINSTER

Georgie Millichamp

Georgie ran a grocery and Blue Cross Animal foods business at Eagle House (the Blue Cross emblem is still on the wall in 1996). He delivered goods in his van around the area. He was an extremely popular person and everyone who knew him in the 1940s and 50s recalls him as a tireless worker for the community. He was continuously organising whist drives, dances and other events for village clubs. Attached is a breakdown of receipts from one dance held in the Old Parish Room in aid of Orleton YFC. Note there were 251 people there 233 having paid 1/6 and 18 paid 1/-. The second sheet shows the total Georgie raised for YFC for the month of September 1951.

Dick Lea from Bicton, locally known as "Disco Dick" played the music for Georgie and later took over his role and provided music for all village dances for some years.

Miracle Cure of Orleton Youth 1948
Leominster advertiser

Coming home on Monday completely cured, is Raymond Fortey, eldest son of Mr. and Mrs. Albert Fortey, of 2 Council Houses. Given three weeks to live, this fifteen year old railway worker has been the subject of a "miracle cure" of tuberculous meningitis – the killer disease.

Until a few months ago there was no known medicine that could be used in its treatment. Then a group of American scientists produced a drug named streptomycin, which owing to the immense difficulties of its preparation, could only be made in minute quantities.

The medical staff at the Queen Elizabeth Hospital, Birmingham, where Raymond was a patient, had only a meagre supply of the drug and more had to be flown from the States during his treatment.

Interviewed at his home after returning with his wife from visiting Raymond, Mr. Fortey told the "Advertiser": "I was told by the medical authorities that the case was absolutely hopeless, but that streptomycin, of which they had a meagre supply would be used. I had never heard of it before. But, I prayed to God that night when I arrived home for I have always believed that He releases miracles far more often than the world realises. And I wondered if this almost untested drug might not be one of them – one of those divine gifts to humanity that from time to time are placed at the disposal of skilled and conscientious men and women as another of his released miracles."

Members of the staff at Woofferton station where Raymond works, collected money to help Mr. and Mrs. Fortey with their travelling expenses to and from the hospital each Wednesday and Sunday, and other gifts received for Raymond include grapes, eggs, fruit, and medicinal wine. This neighbourly spirit has been greatly appreciated by the family as has the kindness shown by the hospital authorities. And now the big excitement that awaits them is Raymond's homecoming next Monday.

Helpers at Youth Club Party 1950s
Back Left to right: Michael Sparey, Len Gough, Ray Fortey, Charlie Ingram, Lily Wilcox, Howard Marshall, Ron Wall.
Middle: Charlie Powles, Bill Palmer, Georgie Millichamp, Miss Preachey, Meg Worthing, Jessie Sparey.
Front: Gladys Fortey, Olive Jones, Mrs. Jones, Christine Kennett, Millicent Morris, Fanny Jones.

Orleton Village 1950s
This photograph shows Eagle House as Georgie Millichamp's Orleton Stores.

Orleton scores a century in Pound Notes

"For the second time in under three months the people of Orleton have raised over £100 for a worthy cause. Last Thursday at a dance and competition organised by Mr. G. H. Millichamp for the benefit of Ray Fortey, the sum of £136-7s-2d was raised. Ray, Orleton and Brimfield CC's wicket keeper suffered permanent injury to his leg in a motor accident last Autumn and his team-mates rallied round to help him.

Prizes in the extremely successful competition were given by Club members. Mr. E. Evans, of Ludlow was commended for the part he played in the competition.

At the carnival dance, held in the Parish Hall, nearly 200 people danced to Millichamp's music, compèred by Mr. A. Marshall Orleton's own "disc jockey". For this dance Messrs. G. Corke, D. Dipper and Millichamp were door stewards and the refreshments were in the hands of Mrs. Price, Mrs. Powles, Mrs. Fortey and Mrs. Worthing.

Mr. J. Vale was steward for the competition in which Miss Francis won a bottle of port, Mr. Preece a box of chocolates, Mr. J. Holland cigarettes and Mr. J. Cadwallader an Easter egg. Mr. & Mrs. S. Griffiths gave a half bottle of whisky and Mr. Griffith's efforts in this competition were instrumental in raising the sum of £5-15s. The prize was won by Mr. Langdon, one of Ray's former workmates.

Other prize-winners at the dance included Miss I. Heapey (lucky door), Mr. R. Smith and Miss J. Skerrett (heads and tails) Mr. M. Cadwallader and Miss S. Dipper (spot waltz).

FREE TRANSPORT. Mr. Millichamp, on behalf of Club members, thanked the dancers for their loyal support and everyone who helped to make the "benefit" such a success. Special mention was made of the three 'bus proprietors' who provided free transport to enable dancers to come from far and wide.

Mr. A. Fortey replying on behalf of his son, said he had not realised before how many friends Ray had in the district. He expressed his sincere thanks to all who had supported the Fund and also those who had sent gifts to Ray while he was in Oswestry Hospital, including the people who had put their cars at the family's disposal in order that they may see their son in his hour of need.

Mrs. Fortey remarked that the success of the Fund was ensured only by the amount of energy and work put into the organisation by Mr. G. H. Millichamp - a remark that brought forth a round of applause.

Several donations were received from people who were unable to attend the dance, and Mr. Marshall auctioned goods to the value of over £4 that well-wishers had given."

Orleton Youth Club outing 1948

Off to Blackpool:- We recognise a few people, Stan Griffiths, Ron Wall, Lily Wilcox, Dennis Edwards, Val Powis, Georgie Millichamp, Talbot Griffiths, Dick Lea, Michael Jones, Audrey Powles, Mary Lewis, Jesse Wood, Marian Jones, Marg Collings, Mrs. Edwards, Trevor Sheppard, Elsie Edwards, Vera Wall, Glenys Sheppard, Violet Reynolds, Mr. Brown, Edie Powles, Gerald Anson, Winnie Duggan, Mr. Duggan, Trevor Jones.

The Old Village Hall area 1964 'Parish Room'

The old Village Hall was situated on the side of the Leominster/Ludlow road in the corner of Portway field. It can be seen in the far left of this photograph. In front of it is the petrol filling station with its small service shop behind. A property has been built on the site and alas the filling station has long since gone. The garden to the right of Fairfield now contains a property, the Fairfield garage has gone and a modern bungalow stands in its place. The orchard to the far right now forms the Village Hall car park and the extended caravan site.

Until 1958 the garage and Fairfield belonged to Mr. Reg Worthing. He kept his buses in the garage and one was used regularly for Georgie's Saturday night dances. The Green Lane "Middleton" housing site was Mr. Worthing's Sawmills. In 1958 however he purchased Woofferton Sawmills and the Green Lane site became his bus depot.

1964 WI Produce Show in the Parish Room

At the end of the room above the door it is possible to see a heart, club, spade and diamond shapes. These used to light at appropriate times during Georgie's Whist Drives.

1964 W.I. Produce Show in the Parish Room

There are a few recognisable faces including Mrs. Rose Manning (Bower Cottage), Margaret Williams (Millbrook Close), Beatrice Radnor (The Folly), and in the foreground a very young Roger Williams. The Room was dismantled in 1965 when the New Village Hall was built.

Old Village Hall (Parish Room) Wedding Breakfast

One of the last wedding breakfasts to take place in the Old Village was that of Ann and Alf Jenkins (Bower House) in 1964. Two members of the family slept in the hall overnight to keep an eye on the place. When it was demolished and removed from Mr. J. M. Sparey's field a fox's lair was discovered beneath.

1963 in the Old Village Hall. John Crofts and Harry Conod taking part in one of their many Fancy Dress escapades.

1970s
Mrs. Rosie Cox with some of her cake creations.

Most villages can boast a handful of talented people within their midst, but an Orleton exhibition proved this North Hereford village has an abundance of skilled residents. The village's second art and craft show filled the parish hall and its annexe on Saturday with everything from pottery and ceramics to paintings and cordon bleu cookery. Throughout the exhibition villagers demonstrated their skills to interest visitors. Dotted between the displays of paintings by Orleton Art Group were straw marquetry and slate drawings, pottery, wood turning, spinning, jewellery making and machine knitting demonstrations. One of the organisers, Margaret Apperley said, "It takes a lot of work to stage this sort of thing, but we feel it has been well worth the effort. Some of the visitors and new people who have moved to the village since our last exhibition couldn't believe there could be so many crafts being done in this area."

November 19th, 1980
Jim and Kitty Collings lived in Orleton for many years. Here they are seen planting a silver birch tree outside the Village Hall watched by the Chairman of the Village Hall Committee Mr. Geoffrey Crofts. Villagers and friends in the background.

Orleton Village Fete 1928

Held on the Glebe Land Orleton. "Four Dancers" including Margaret Apperley left and Beattie Radnor right.

Nitty Gritty Shindig being opened by Hereford United player Billy Tucker. Alf Jenkins on the right welcomes the guest. Seated on the platform (farm trailer to be more exact) from L to R:- Linda Burton, Mr. Michael Sparey (Committee Chairman), Mr. & Mrs. Harry Conod (judges of the competitions).

Orleton Fete 1973 called the Nitty Gritty Shindig

This was the first fete to be held after the 'New' Village Hall opened. A parade began from the Boot and was organised by Alf Jenkins.

1973 Fete. Competition up to 10 years class of Fancy Dress

Included in this group are left to right:- Sian Evans, Graham Jenkins, Granny Jenkins, Helen Jenkins, Paul Morgan, The Deakin girls, Mrs. Deakin, Adrian Sparey, Kate Sparey, Edie Radnor, Janice Butcher, Sybil Griffiths, Adrian West, Vera Lloyd, Greville Lewis, Alistair Lewis, Carol Lewis, David Lewis.

Orleton Fete July 1973

(From Ludlow Advertiser Report) "The Nitty Gritty Shindig held at Orleton on Saturday was a great success. The event was opened by Hereford centre half Billy Tucker. One of the afternoon's highlights was the colourful fancy dress parade. Winners were Simon and Dylan Worthing and Andrew Williams. Childrens' sports were organised by Geoff Crofts. Orleton Brownies organised various competitions and a Clay pigeon shoot was also held in the evening. Dolly Ducking proved to be a favourite game with a bevy of dollies, blonde, brunette and redheads to duck. Every dolly ducked was a shilling in the coffers of Orleton Village Hall Committee and there was no shortage of triers.

First in the water was Sue Plant whose complacency was shattered within quarter of an hour of the opening. Sue Holland, Ruth Morris and Rosemary Cox were three other volunteers in this up to date version of the ducking stool. The rules were simple - ring the bell with a ball and duck your dolly in a tank of cold water.

The event catered for everyone from toddlers to OAPs. Miss Isobel Porter reputed to be 81, had her first ride in a model T. Ford racing car, one of the stable owned by enthusiast Mr. Reg Worthing of the Spout House.

The recreation Ground was packed and every organisation using the Village Hall helped boost hall funds by contributing some attraction to the day."

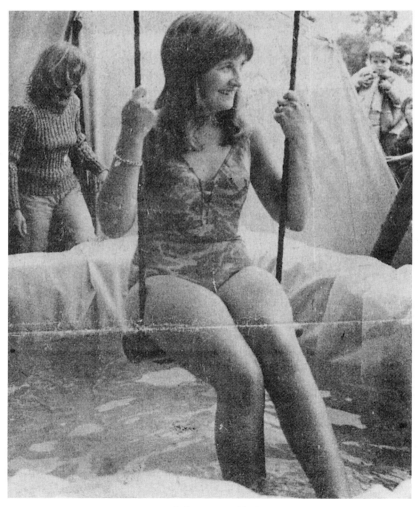

Orleton Fete 1973
Rosemary Cox sitting pretty - before the plunge.

Orleton Fete 1973
One of the volunteers just hitting the water (Ruth Morris?) and ouch was it cold?

1978 Village Hall Fete
Having a pony and cart ride with Margaret Evans are Mary Worthing, Carol Fox and others.

Orleton Fiesta 1978

'Games involved gallons of water, sawdust and some not too fresh eggs; all part of the fun day at Orleton Fiesta. The highlight of the afternoon's activities was the "It's a Knockout" competition in which six teams entered into the high spirited antics centred around a swimming pool.

The teams taking part were the Maidenhead, Football Club, Youth Club, Cooper Team and the Village Hall Team. The winners The Football Club were presented with a shield and a gallon of cider by Mr. Stan Lloyd. He organised the event with helpers Michael and Roger Sparey. Henry, Michael, John and Geoffrey Lewis provided the equipment. Earlier in the day there had been a Go-cart race from Kitchen Hill. It nearly ended in disaster when three of the vehicles collided.

The sun shone throughout the day and a large crowd was attracted. Over £400 was taken during the afternoon. The event culminated with a disco in the Village Hall provided by Berrington Road Show.'

Fiesta 1978. Go-cart Race through Village

Drivers left to right:- Simon Holland, Shaun Jennings, Roger Williams. The pushers are Nichola Holland, Mike Saunders, John Williams, Nick Aldridge.

Village Hall Fiesta 1978
Under 6 section for fancy dress. *From Left to Right:-* Kate Plant, Paul Faulkner, Debbie Cox, Sarah Cox, Helen Morris, Karen Jenkins, Ashley Douglas.

Village Hall Fete 1978
One of the first fetes to be held on the Recreation Ground. This is obviously the W.I. stall. Among those to be seen are Millicent Godding, Olive Postons, Rosie Cox, Chris Ellis, the back of Derek Saunders and the Snape Family in the far background.

Orleton Fiesta 1978. Fancy dress class for the over 6s.
Group includes Samantha Gillum, Graham Jenkins, Duncan Morgan, Helen Jenkins, Rebecca Snape, Helen Harris.

1980s Assembly of Orleton Fete Carnival Parade near Ye Olde House.
Clare Sheppard on left and Ann Jenkins as Orleton's answer to Hilda Ogden.

Public Houses

The Maidenhead Inn

The property was built in the 17th Century with a later stone addition and was known as a Court House in 1800. It has undergone several structural changes over the years. Like other public houses in the area it was initially a cider house, and then a cider and beer house until the 1950s, and of course is now licenced to sell wines and spirits.

It was the headquarters of the Independent Order of Oddfellows for many years, and it seems to have had a number of wheelwrights who were also publicans as well. It is known that in the early part of this century Joseph Hughes, the landlord, was a wheelwright. So was a certain gentleman by the name of Pearce in 1912.

Two Fairs were held regularly in Orleton, one was the Hiring Fair and Horse Fair and this was held in the centre of the village in King's Road. However, another Fair took place in April in the meadow in front of The Maidenhead at which Hereford Cattle were sold.

Late 1940s. Hetty Bloom and daughter with Mr. Sam Pound of Lower Tower Hill (Still Water Cott in the 1990s), standing outside the Maidenhead. Hetty's father Mr. Stephens was the landlord of the Maidenhead.

Maidenhead Inn Coronation Day 1911.

Maidenhead Inn
Orleton Band outside the Maidenhead Inn early this century. The dog doesn't seem to have been disturbed by the music.

Maidenhead Inn 1917
This photograph includes Mr. & Mrs. Pearce and their daughter standing by the door.

Maidenhead Inn 1927

Mr. & Mrs. Bert Bowen and Mrs. Bowen's sister are standing by the BP petrol pumps. Observers may have noticed that the public house sign has been moved since earlier photographs.

Mr. & Mrs. Bert Bowen (relations of Mrs. Ivy Bowen) were landlord and landlady of The Bay Horse. Mr. Bowen was very amiable. Mr. Jim Ingram recalls that in the 1930s he and other lads would go to St. George's for Sunday Evensong, then call at The Bay Horse, where, because they were slightly under age, Mr. Bowen would say, "Yes my boys you may have one half pint only." Jim said they would pay their 2d then walk on to Richards Castle to meet their girlfriends. Later of course they would have to walk back to Orleton.

Inside the Maidenhead 1950s.

Left to Right:- Mr. Bob Brick, ..., Mr. Stephens behind the bar, his daughter Hetty Bloom, *and far right* Mr. Tom Apperley.

Maidenhead Corner 1950s.
On the right hand side the
round, yellow 'AA' mileage
sign read '139 miles to
London'.

Maidenhead Corner.
A more recent photograph. Part of the building has been demolished to improve visibility of the main road.

The Boot Inn

An early 17th Century half timber construction Public House with a stone tile roof to this section and a later brick built wing to the South. Formerly three properties as can be seen from the photographs displayed here.

The main half timbered section to the North having been one of the many drinking houses in the village, the centre section was reputedly a milliner's and the southerly section was, until the middle of this century, a butcher's shop.

The entrance into the main part of the Pub was moved from the front elevation to the side and a stone tiled porch was constructed early in this century when the chimney that is evident in the photographs was removed. Another fireplace was built in the other corner of this section but with recent modernisation this has also been removed. In the centre section the modernisation programme exposed the large inglenook fireplace which is now used. Unfortunately in the modernisation an 18th century oak chest was removed, this used to form a trap door into the cellar and many visitors had a shock when it was pointed out to them as they often used to sit on it, unaware of the danger below.

To the rear of the property, one of the few remaining single cell dwellings remains, with a fairly modern asbestos sheeted roof protecting it from the weather. Hopefully this will be restored in the not too distant future.

Kelly's Directory of 1861 reports that "The Court Moor Park Lodge of Ancient Order of Foresters" meet at the Boot Inn. This no longer happens but does anyone know when this Lodge ceased?

1940s. Village near The Boot Inn.
We wish we could read the menu. Note G. H. Millichamp's Stores on the right.

The Boot Inn

Last month's Grapevine carried an article about the Manor House, probably the most substantial building in our village. We can also claim what is said to be the smallest dwelling-house in the county. Next time you are passing The Boot, look over the garden wall towards the rear of the Inn and you will see a small timber-framed building which can be mistaken for an out-house, but which is in fact a one-time occupied dwelling.

The building is roughly nine feet square, with a gabled roof which now has a modern covering. The original would doubtless be tiled. The timber framework of the whole structure is certainly authentic and it is particularly interesting to see how the joints have been pegged together, the peg-heads being left proud of the timbers. There is no damp-course, in fact the structure appears to have been raised on wooden 'sleepers' - baulks of timber layed at ground level, and is still largely of split laths plastered with mud, re-inforced with hay or straw. I have seen the house referred to as a 'one cell' building, which would mean that as built, there would be just one room, in which all domestic activities would happen. Now it looks as if the roof space has been floored and a sort of stair-way put in, doubtless to create separate sleeping accommodation.

I suppose the house dates from much about the same time as The Boot itself ... Perhaps some future proprietor may be interested enough to make something of the little house.

(Extract from an article in the October 1983 edition of The Grapevine by Mr. G. Platt.)

The Boot Inn 1960

A tale hangs by the sign of The Boot which dominates the front of the public house. The idea came from an old door-stop. Imagination and craftsmanship account for the rest. The co-author was asked to print a new sign representing a cobbler in 1991. This only hung for two years then the old boot sign once again replaced it.

The Boot Inn 1920

A number of changes have taken place both inside and outside The Boot Inn since this was taken; but the one yew tree is still there. The new war memorial can be seen and in the distance opposite Kitchen Hill house the oak tree so many of us remember.

The Village Stores and Post Office is about half its present size. A shed stood at the far end and the cottage on this side was a farm worker's cottage which later belonged to Inchmoor farm.

Mine hosts
Bob and Rita West
at The Boot Inn 1978.

Granny Bedford, proprietor of
The Bay Horse 1930's.

The Bay Horse

Alf Jenkins first became acquainted with Orleton in the 1950s when he played in a darts' match arranged between his home, The Dhu Stone Inn Clee Hill and The Bay Horse. Jack and Ivy Bowen always made the team most welcome and Alf's father said Ivy's infectious laugh was something special. Ivy could certainly have written a best seller about her fun and experiences as a licencee. Sadly The Bay Horse ceased to be a public house in 1974 when the Bowens retired.

Miscellaneous

Early 1900s
The Orr Family at the Bower.

1905. Kathy Passey with a fox cub. It had been dug out by Col. Hill on the Manor land and Kathy reared and kept it as a pet.

1902. The Passey family ready for an outing. The photograph was taken in Tunnel Lane (near the home of Mr. & Mrs. Underwood 1990s)

Orleton 'First World War Boys'
(1914-1918)

War Memorial 1919
Left Harry Passey and Right Ted
Hughson with others at the
Memorial.

Orleton and Brimfield Homeguard

They used to meet in Orleton Parish Room. Colonel Hill from the Manor was in charge of the platoon. It was transported by Ray Holt in his open-sided coach. Ray's father John was the last blacksmith at Orleton Forge.

A manoeuvre competition was held at New Radnor between all the Home Guard platoons of the area. The photograph was taken because Orleton and Brimfield had top marks. Due to Colonel Hill's influence the platoon was extremely well turned out.

The authors were told one humorous story about an occasion when Brimfield were attacking Orleton via Tunnel Lane. Jack Francis was being challenged when someone inadvertently gave him the pass word. With that the contingent walked straight through Orleton lines. Unfortunately Joe Vale (a well known barman at The Boot) was injured twice on the same day. Firstly he lobbed a hand grenade but as he moved rapidly forward it came down and hit him on the forehead. A few minutes later someone thrust a .303 through the hedge and took a small chunk out of his cheek.

The photograph includes:- Left to Right Back Row, Jack Jones, Bill Humphries, Ernie Ingram, John Lowe, Bob Cound.

Middle Row. Jack Francis, Geoff Vale, Mobbie Nottingham, Phil Postons, Jim Maund, Tom Dyer, Bill Morgan.

Front Row. Bert Fortey, Maurice Samuels, Joe Vale, Tom Apperley, Ray Holt, Bob Jones, Ern Morris, Dave Williams.

A family at the Goggin in the 1920s pose for a photograph in their Sunday best.

Orleton Band 1928-29

Back L to R:- Mr. Price, Tom Dyer, Mortimer Price, ..., ...,
Middle:- Ray Holt, Sid Holt, Harry Passey, Bill Cleeton. *Front:*- Roland Vale, ..., Artie Powis, Jack Williams.

Mr. Passey lived in Tunnel Lane Cottage. Opposite in the field and next to the road was a small shed. This was Mr. Passey's cobblers shop. Here small group band practises took place every week. When Jim Collings, Jim Porter and Jimmy Wall arrived, Mr. Passey would always say, "Have a glass of cider boys before you begin." He seemed to think it would make them play better.

Honeymoon Cottage, the Post Office part of our Village Stores was a cottage until recent years. Many people including Ray Holt, Artie Powis and Harry Passey spent their honeymoon at this cottage, lived there for a little time then moved on. As a result it was known locally as "Honeymoon Cottage."

Chapel House Garden 1935

View from the house when it was a chapel. The cottage at the end is Miss Maynard's (1996). Beyond is an open space where Mr. & Mrs. Bertinat's house is. Through the gate behind the trees is the 'Dead house'. The wheel bier, which was used from the chapel to Brook Hall graveyard was housed in this building. The 'Dead house' still stands in the Bertinat's garden and may be seen if you walk down the Boot Lane. It was known by this name because Mr. Jim Collings' father dropped dead in the wheel bier house. Mrs. Collings and Marg are seen in the photograph.

Alice Wall and Turk lived at No. 1 Church Lane in the 1940s. She used to keep magpies and spent considerable time teaching them to talk. Locals recall that some of these birds acquired a considerable vocabulary.

George Handley at No. 1 Church Lane (1940s). Well Cottage in the background

Geoff Fuller's lorry at the Bower in the 1940s. He often washed his lorry in the ford at Millbrook. His home was Orchard Cottage and occasionally he penned his sheep and cattle up in the middle of Church Lane.

Orleton Outing to Barry Island.
Front L to R:- Reg Grosvenor, Alf Sparey, Dave Williams.   *Back:-* Jim Rogers, Tom Delahay.

Little Billy Hince

When Ted Hughson was living at Orleton Residential Home (The Old Vicarage) he informed us that Billy Hince delivered bread for Shinglers of Ashford. However, he also said that Little Billy delivered with Ernest Grafton who lived at The Halletts and worked for Vaughan's Bakery, The Old Mill.

Billy was killed on the main A49 whilst on his rounds. He was hit by a vehicle. This must have been an unfortunate accident because there would have been very little traffic in those days.

THE RESIDENCE

Church House as presented in the sale catalogue when the house and farm was sold in the 1940s. Note the open fields in the background.

Taken on Church House lawns in the 1940s. Claremont can be seen in the background.

This group is celebrating the christening of Charles Roberts, grandson of Mr. Herbert who lived at Church House. Mr. and Mrs. Roberts and baby Charles can be seen in the centre of the picture. Many of you will remember Mr. Roberts when he ran 'Roberts Ironmongers Shop' in Ludlow's Broad Street. Charles of course ran 'Beards' the very successful wallpaper and paint shop in Upper Galdeford, Ludlow for many years.

William Herbert, Church House 1940s.

Church Lane early 1950s.
Well Cottages in the background. Dennis Edwards and helper unloading timber.

Dr. Geoffrey Vaughan with his twins Gaye and Paul outside their home, Orleton House in the 1950s. Dr. Geoff was in partnership with his father, locally known as 'Old Dr. Vaughan'. Dr. Geoffrey's family was well known in rugby circles. He emigrated to New Zealand.

1950s. Rev. Vivian Jones, his wife Joyce and son Paul enjoying a quiet drink with Mary Worthing.

Mr. R. R. Worthing

Reg Worthing was a character, like Georgie Millichamp who Orleton people should remember with gratitude.

He was a parish Councillor, District Councillor, Chairman of District Council, School Governor and a business man with a flair. He worked extremely hard to ensure Orleton was not left behind and had amenities second to none. He was one of the prime instigators in helping to obtain a new school, village hall, sewerage scheme, mains water and street lighting.

Reg Worthing's first new home in Orleton was at Fairfield. The buses he owned were housed and serviced in a garage behind the property. This photograph taken from the roadside shows Reg's wife Mary and Remus their dog. In the distance stands one of the coaches. The garage remained Mr. Worthing's until 1958 when The Patrick Family purchased it. The land on the photograph then became a caravan park.

Mechanics Ken Evans and Tom Nottingham in Mr. Reg Worthing's garage at Fairfield in the 1950s.

Mr. Worthing's bus parked by Fairfield filling station in the 1950s. The Maidenhead Inn can be seen in the right background.

A Worthing's vehicle parked at Fairfield advertising his luxury coaches. The Parish Room can be seen in the background. The filling station forecourt was often used unofficially as extra parking space during Parish Room functions.

1950s Central Cafe Leominster. This was R. R. Worthing's travel bureau and booking office. Here we see Mr. Jim Ingram and Mr. Stan Griffiths. Both were employees for this firm for many years, Jim joining it when he was demobbed in the 1940s.

In 1958 Mr. Worthing's sawmills on the site opposite Tower Hill in Green Lane became his bus depot. He purchased Woofferton Sawmills. This photograph shows Mr. Jack Evason at Woofferton. In the background is the crane framework which was demolished in 1996.

Bromyard Show 1977
Mr. R.R. Worthing of Spout House with his Model T Ford Tourer. It won the Pilkington Memorial Challenge Cup. On the left is Mr. Edgar Pilkington, organiser of the Show's veteran car section. In the middle is Mr. Worthing's grandson Dylan holding a miniature cup.

Bert Fortey (1910-1993)

Alf first met Bert Fortey as a member of Orleton Parish Council in 1964.

He lived in Orleton for many years and spent much of his life working in the agricultural industry. He had very definite principles to which he vehimently adhered but he heeded the opinions of others and genuinely respected those who thought differently.

Bert founded Orleton branch of the Agricultural Workers' Union in 1946, was secretary for 36 years, chairman of Kingsland branch, a county delegate and delegate at annual conferences. On one occasion he said "My parents were like peasants on the land and were treated like dirt and that's why I joined the union. Trying to improve the conditions under which farmworkers work has been an important part of my life. Much has been achieved in the past thirty years, notably seeing the Tied Cottage Bill pass through Parliament. That is something for which I have fought very strenuously and which

Gladys and Bert Fortey being made Life Members of Leominster and District Gardening Club in May 1990.

will be for the long term good of the farming industry".

Behind Bert's fight for legislation had been his own experience of threatened eviction. After refusing to do overtime in the evening of a day off Bert was sacked. "It was a terrible experience not only for me but for my wife and young children, but, if things are better for the agricultural worker when I leave this life than when I came into it, the hard work will have been worthwhile."

As well as being a Parish Councillor he was a magistrate for 15 years and when he went to live in Leominster he became the first President of the town's gardening club. With others he worked very hard to lay plans for Orleton's new school.

Bert's one regret was that he couldn't afford to "wed my lovely wife in church but had to cycle to Leominster Registry Office instead".

Mr. Bert Fortey with the Agricultural Workers' Union Banner.

Orleton Farmworkers and friends off on a sea-side outing in the 1950s. Picture includes:- Stan Griffiths, Frank Saunders, Ted Thomas, Mr. Oakley (Landlord of The Boot) Jack Duncalfe, Charlie Randall and Harry Davies.

Corvedale Motors
Mr. Bert Fortey and Mr. Stan Griffiths (Driver) await arrival of Farmworkers for their outing. 1950s.

Mrs. Margaret Apperley

A very special person. She spent her childhood at Broad Green with sister Beryl. She was for many years a supply teacher in the area, later marrying Fred Apperley and moving to Church House Farm where her children Sue, Jim and David were born.

We cannot think of any noteable organisation in which she did not participate. We doubt whether our present school or our new vicarage would have materialised without her determination and energy.

She was a very skilful Parish Councillor and we all benefited from her wisdom. Her motto was "Surely we can solve this problem by having a chat with so and so - much better than sending a letter".

Margaret Apperley was a real christian; other peoples' worries, apprehensions and anxieties were hers. No matter how busy she was she would help. Many Y.F.C. members have been given inspiration to display, or create a flower arrangement by Margaret.

The staff, school, governors and past parents of the three parishes will always be endebted to Margaret.

She was an artist with flowers. Her creations for our flower festivals were joys to behold.

We are so pleased she is acknowledged in our church by the altar rail designed and made by local craftman Patrick Faulkner.

We cannot forget you Margaret; a dear friend, we still miss you very much.

Margaret and Fred Apperley at the christening of their grandson Robin Moss in 1989.

An article in the Grapevine, January 1984 by Margaret Apperley
The Boot Inn in times Past

Our editor for the month has suggested that a topical subject for a Grapevine article might be The Boot Inn, so I have done my best to unearth a few memories in a very short space of time.

It seems that about 70 years ago a Mrs. Lawrence was the landlady of the beer and cider house as it was then, but the first people I hazily remember were a Mr. & Mrs. Webb.

In addition to the pub they did a little farming, keeping several cows in the building at the back, also having land at Stone Green, Little Overton, which I believe Sid Nicholls may have had later.

George Handley (Bower Cottage) was employed by them to help generally.

The Webbs also ran the village taxi, a large square black Ford 80 I'm told, which ferried people to and from Woofferton Junction and also Leominster.

The driver of this vehicle was Bill Edwards, the eldest brother of Ernie and Sidney.

Very early photographs show the front door of The Boot right by the pavement where there is now a lounge window.

There was of course no water or electricity - a pump stood by the back door and oil lamps and candles lit the building. I'm told that Mr. Webb with his candle at the door in snowy weather, provided the local boys in the opposite hedge with target practise. Whose snowball could extinguish the candle? Boys were boys even then.

The cider sold at this time was made locally, much of it at 'Claremont', home of the Prices, a much respected family, the three brothers being stonemasons and a sister the postmistress.

It was of course 'rough' cider and not very sweet. It is said that one regular customer was heard to say, "Sharn't I be glad when I've had enough".

There was just one bar at this time but the landlord allowed the use of the sitting room for Oddfellows meetings and football committees.

The Webbs had three daughters, one of whom, Daisy, married Jim Gale, who ran the butcher's shop at the Boot. This was in the front room next to the lane, the door facing the road inside the boundary wall with a paled gate. The slaughter house was at the back of the building.

Animals were sometimes bought in Leominster market and Harry George who worked for the Gales brought them home. Usually it was a solitary heifer and apparently Harry was very grateful if he could join other animals travelling this way. Otherwise one heifer had a habit of hedge hopping and poor Harry travelled twice the distance chasing it.

Eventually the Webbs retired and changed houses with the Gales going to live at Bank House with their daughter Lil who some of you will remember as Mrs. Warburton.

Harry George delivered meat on his bicycle - one lady to this day remembers the snowy whiteness of the cloth which lined the basket.

The Gales left the village for the Hereford area, having sold out to the Byngs who still employed George Handley as general factotum. Harry George had joined the forces as it was wartime. At this time I'm told the Boot flourished partly due to the presence of American Servicemen being stationed at Berrington Park. They walked up Tunnel Lane to sample the beer and cider.

I understand it was also at this time that the two small rooms adjacent to the garden were joined, a steel girder replacing the weight bearing wall between.

I think the Oakleys came after the Byngs, Mr. Oakley being a brother of Phyllis Nicholls of Little Overton. They opened the first lounge or 'Cocktail Bar' as it was called in place of the butcher's shop which was relegated to the rear room, soon closing its doors. The spirit licence was obtained by the Oakleys. It was probably during the Oakley's time that Joe Vale joined the staff.

Several owners, none staying long until Dasher Downing took charge of the premises. He planned the lounge, Philip Postons replacing the steel girder with oak and generally placing a craftsman's mark upon the place. The cocktail bar now became the dining room.

The Boot received some notoriety when the landlord forcibly removed the hat of our village constable who called somewhat inconveniently after time one night.

The daily papers carried a picture of Dasher resplendent with parrot on shoulder and though he was fined for his misdeed he considered that the publicity had been more than worth it.

And so to the Gambles the last owners, the connection of Proctor and Gamble who extended the dining room by way of the stone archway which was built by Philip Postons.

I was told to write about the past but the Boot was really put on the map by Bob and Rita West in the 70s when people came from far and wide to sample their excellent food in the restaurant.

Thank you to Bill Ingram, Ernie Edwards, Philip Postons and Rosemary Jones who gave me much of the above information.

The building of Council Houses Green Lane 1954

This was on land formerly known as The Allotments. These were a series of large garden plots for the use of the villagers. The bungalows were built on an old orchard site. A high hedge which bordered Green Lane was felled.

11th August, 1960

Age and youth walk side by side along the main street of Orleton. Mr. Samuel Brooks, aged 85, takes 6 year old John Underwood, the son of Mr. Brooks' niece, on one of their many strolls.

A 1960s photograph of Phil Postons, a craftsman Orleton can be proud of. His work has included the making of doors for some of our Hereford churches. Here Phil is seen shaping another tribute to his career.

1990s - A dream come true.

P. H. Postons is a well respected and established building firm. Like his father before him, Phil was the local undertaker. He is a first class craftsman and his work can be seen in so many places throughout our local communities. In latter years Phil and his son Chris have specialised in building. Phil is seen here in his modern, well equipped workshop. I'm sure he would say that it is a dream come true as he reflects on all the work they had to do by hand years ago.

George and Mary Postons (grandparents to Phil) first lived at "The Bellows Cottage' (top of Hunt's Lane) in 1885. George worked at The Lodge Farm. They subsequently moved over to Waterloo House at Orleton Common. One of their seven children, Harry, left school to work at first in a timber merchant's yard for a short time before becoming an apprentice carpenter and joiner, also doing wheelwrighting and undertaking under the supervision of Joseph Hughes who ran a small business from a workshop at Fairfield House opposite The Maidenhead on the site of the present Fairfield caravan park.

Harry Postons completed his apprenticeship and worked for several years for Mr. Hughes before he decided in 1912 to start his own business at Croft End, Little Overton. He had only been in business for two years when The Great War started, and because he was already a Territorial soldier was literally given a few hours to pack his kit, (including tools) and *march* with his comrades to Shrewsbury Barracks. He became a Staff Sergeant and was demobbed in 1919. Sadly his first wife died of influenza in the epidemic of 1918 leaving him with a two year old daughter, Hilda.

After his War service he restarted business again at No. 2 Chapel Terrace (the middle of the then three cottages) with a workshop situated across the road in the orchard. In 1922 he married Lizzie Jane and they had two children whilst living at Chapel Terrace (Philip and Arthur). Harry wanted to expand his business and bought in 1930 a black and white cottage called Yew Tree Cottage next to Church House Farm which he subsequently renamed 'Woodcote' where the present owner, Harry's third son, Ken, was born and still lives. The curved corrugated roof workshop was moved lock stock and barrel to the orchard and has remained there ever since, although in 1990 it had to be upgraded to meet modern standards.

Harry's eldest son, Philip, joined the family firm from school and managed the business through the early War years until his father died in 1944. Phil continued to manage the business with his mother until 1950 and then took over as the proprietor.

In 1945 Phil married Olive and in 1946 moved into what was then called 'Corner House' (which is now the Post Office end of the Village Stores). Here three children were brought up until they went to live at No. 10 Green Lane in 1954. In 1964 Phil built his own home which was the first privately owned house to be built in Orleton for nearly 100 years (Council houses and bungalows excluded).

Phil's son Chris, started his apprenticeship with the family firm in 1962 and in 1973 became a partner, and he and his wife, Kate, have continued running the business ever since. Chris and Kate presently live at 'Orchard House' Church Lane with their sons, John and Michael, who are the fifth generation of Postons to live in Orleton.

The Bower 1962
The Butcher family in front of No. 1 and 2 The Bower (now called The Bower). Note the old brick wall and the large apple tree. Lil Collins off to get water from Dicken's Lane.

Church Lane 1962
Part of the Butcher family, Janice, Eric, Gaynor and Hilary with Mrs. Butcher's mother.

June 1972. Four generations at Orleton
Mr. Jim Sparey of Oakleigh, Portway celebrating his 80th birthday at a village hall party. Mr. Jim Sparey is sitting in the middle. On the right is Mr. Bill Sparey of Broad Farm, Leominster (son) and on the left is Mr. Richard Sparey (grandson) and Timothy (great grandson). The Sparey family has lived in Orleton for over 50 years. Mr. Jim Sparey, born in Presteigne was a real inspiration to Orleton Methodists for many years.

Orleton Playgroup 1973

Easter Bonnet Parade. *The group includes* Mrs. Minnie Conod, Robina Lloyd, Karen Jenkins, Rachael Lewer, The Albrow Twins, Helen Morris, Nick Turner, Jill Francis, Lucinda Lloyd, Lara Conod, Debbie Cox, James Hunt, Robert Davies.

Plant a Tree in 73
Mrs. Mollie Bowen, Chairman of Orleton Parish Council being assisted by Mr. Fred Apperley (Parish Councillor) to plant a silver birch near Mill Brook. In the background are Graham Jenkins, Sue Apperley and David Apperley taking an interest. Also looking on are Sybil Griffiths and Ena Sparey.

Plant a Tree in 73
W.I. and Parish Council plant a tree near the brook at the end of Mill Lane. *L to R:-* Alf Jenkins (Parish Councillor), Mrs. Baker, Mrs. Capp-Davies, Mrs. Olive Postons, David and Sue Apperley, Graham Jenkins, Mr. Fred Apperley (Parish Councillor), Mr. Reg Worthing (District Councillor), Mrs. Sylvia Apperley, Mrs. Nora Marsh, Miss Sybil Griffiths, hidden Ena Sparey, Mrs. Meg Worthing, Mr. Richmond Owens and dog, Mrs. Margaret Apperley (Parish Councillor), Mr. Reynolds.

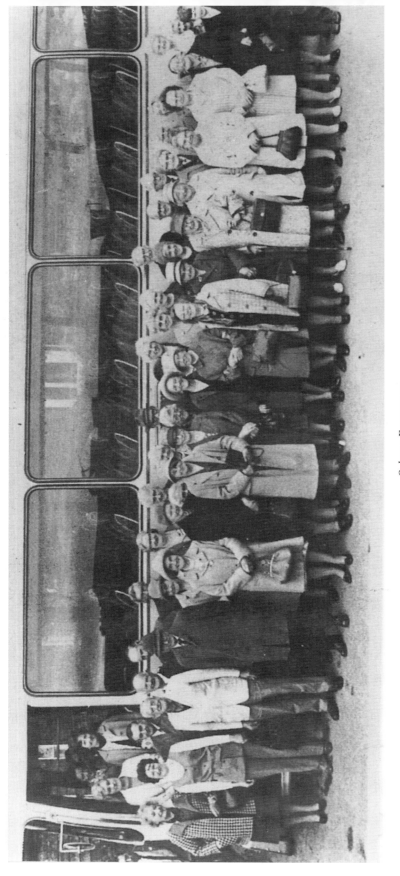

Orleton Evergreens

Orleton Evergreens began in the 1970s under the leadership of Mrs. Meg Worthing (Spout House). In 1996 it is still thriving with Joan Edwards Inchmoor as leader.

This photograph shows the Club embarking on a mystery trip. In those days Ade Sparey always went as mascot.

On the bus steps are:- Meg Worthing with helpers. Eileen Morris and Joan Edwards. *In front are* Sybil Griffiths and Sylvia Sparey.

Left to Right Back Row:- Donald Lloyd, Mr. Brooks, Mr. Evans, Ern Ingram, Mrs. Vaughan, Mrs. Evans, Mrs. Loxton, Mr. J. Sparey, Mrs. J. Sparey, Mrs. K. Stokes, ..., ..., ..., Mr. Hall, ..., ..., ..., ..., ...,
....

Front:- Mr. Morgan, Richmond Owens, Isobel Porter, ..., ..., Mrs. Rose Manning, ..., ..., Mrs. Parton, Miss Isherwood, Granny Griffiths, ..., Miss Young, Mrs. Capp-Davis, ..., Sissie Price, ..., Ethel Davis, Mrs. Hall, Mrs. Philips, Mrs. Powell, Mrs. Conod, Ade Sparey.

Mrs. Mollie Bowen. Chairman of Orleton Parish Council in 1980.

Mrs. Joan Edwards - Inchmoor. Leader of The Evergreens in 1980 and still the leader in 1996.

1980. Mrs. Edna Bertinat. Chairman of Orleton Art Club. It was set up in 1975 and has presented many exhibitions in the area. The Club still flourishes in the 1990s and examples of its members' work are always on display at the Doctors' Surgery to brighten your visit.

1980. Mr. Brightly, the proprietor of The village Stores.

Orleton Tile Factory Opens

Ludlow Advertiser Report

Orleton Manor. "Emily and Bobby Jones proprietors of the tile factory which has opened at Orleton Manor, give a round of applause to Chairman of Cosira, David Davenport at the official opening last week.

Their tile making business - in a converted barn - has made a flying start. The enterprise, supported by the Council for small industries in Rural Areas, is turning out hand painted copies of 18th century wall tiles and the finished article is going down a storm in America.

Jones Tiles, established by Robert Jones, now employs seven in the old tithe barn at the Manor. He moved from Leintwardine two years ago, taking over the 75th redundant building to receive grant aid from Cosira. He began by making copies of 18th century Delft tiles, the familiar blue tiles with rural scenes described within a circle. He now has a range of 200 tiles which include some of his own designs using the same techniques of hand glazing, painting and finishing as the five inch copies of Delft scenes.

More than 150,000 tiles are made each year, most of them going to the American market. With improved production facilities Mr. Jones is now developing the home market.

The workshop was officially opened by David Davenport Chairman of Cosira and he unveiled a plaque on the barn wall. The workshop houses a glazing room, drying facilities, a design and hand painting studio, a firing kiln room, showroom and offices.

Woofferton Junction

We are including a few notes about Woofferton because the junction was extremely important to the agricultural community of Orleton.

Woofferton:- Kelly's directory of Shropshire 1891.

"4 miles south of Ludlow is the township with a junction station of the Tenbury branch of the Great Western Railway with the Shrewsbury and Hereford joint Railway. Adjoining the railway station are the timber yards and a large steam sawmill of Messrs. Barrow (Barlow) and Sons of Wimslow, employing about 20 hands in the conversion of English timber for which the district is celebrated.

The mission room here, opened in 1890, is a building in the Shrewsbury Cottage Style with black and white oak framing on a brick foundation; it affords sittings for 160 persons. The west end is used as a working mens' club and reading room. It is well supplied with periodicals and weekly papers; the site and building were the sole gift of Mrs. and Miss Foster of Moor Park."

Mr. Graham Nottingham informed us that the Hereford-Shrewsbury Railway Co. opened the line for goods only on July 30th 1852, the first passengers being carried on December 6th 1853. The building contractors were Thomas Brazey and William Field who were also to build for the Tenbury Railway Co., the Tenbury Link which opened on September 1st 1861.

In 1858 the Kington/Stourport Canal had closed between Woofferton and Leominster and was bought by the Hereford/Shrewsbury Railway Co. who drained it. The Tenbury Railway Co. did likewise to their section when it was purchased on September 5th 1860.

Woofferton was a very important junction for the transportation of produce from Orleton farms to the North and Midlands in particular.

The Manor Farm and Portway were two of many farms which took their cherry crop there to be eventually sold in Manchester.

Mr. Reg Grosvenor from Comberton recalls that most sheep farmers sent fleeces via rail too.

Mr. Alf Sparey remembers at least six dairy farmers including his father Jim from Portway taking 17 gallon churns across the track, loading them into trucks and bringing empties for next day's milk. Mr. Herbert of Church House Farm sent cider regularly from the junction and Mr. Jim Sparey used to bring empty casks back for him. Cattle and sheep were regularly sent and brought to Woofferton.

Sugar beet was an important crop especially during war time and a large tonnage went from Woofferton via the Tenbury Link to Kidderminster to be manufactured into sugar.

Mr. Jack Bowen from The Bay Horse and other coal merchants relied on Woofferton for their supplies.

The junction created other industries, including the Sawmills and a Shell Mex and BP Depot.

In spite of the fact that an horrendous fire completely destroyed the Sawmills in the 1930s it restarted again and still continues in the 1990s.

This photograph was produced by Mrs. Win. Faulkner. It is taken looking from the junction towards the Orleton/Salwey road (the middle of Oreton Building Supplies timber yard in the 1990s).

The railway cottages on the left are little changed. In the centre four gentlemen are standing in front of "The Refreshment Rooms." For many years these were run by the Moulton family of the Salwey Arms. It was a licenced premises and locally known as "Abraham's Bosom." Mrs. Ivy Bowen worked there as barmaid for nine years during the 1930s. She recalls it as a very happy episode of her life. She said her future hubby Jack often popped in when collecting coal and she took him along regularly to church services in the Mission Room.

She also remembers the considerable influx of fruit pickers who came annually from South Wales by rail to Woofferton. They stayed in the area for weeks and increased the sales at the "Bosom" considerably.

As a small child Mrs. Winnie Faulkner lived at Mill Brook House Orleton (home of Mrs. Nora Marsh in the 1990s). Her father, Mr. Clark was a business man trading in fruit amongst other things. He owned the shop on the right of the photograph. It is possible to discern 'Clarks' above the door. This was a general provisions and fruit shop and at the rear there was a cafe. This provided a welcome cup of tea and refreshments for railway passengers. The building still remains in the 1990s and is Oreton Building Supplies DIY shop and office.

The Tenbury line to Woofferton was a very important link to the Midlands but it also enabled children to travel from the Tenbury area via Woofferton to Leominster and Ludlow Grammar Schools.

Many rural railway lines closed in the 1960s under the Beeching axe and on the 31st July 1961 the Tenbury Link closed too.

Mr. Graham Nottingham reminds us that the spelling for the station was not consistent even in the 1930s. The name board called it Woofferton, the signal box Wofferton and the platform trolleys Wooferton.

Woofferton Junction. Date unknown. The gentleman nearest the lamp standard is Mr. Will Penny, who lived at Hayfield, Brimfield. His son Len Penny ran the local taxi service for many years.

Woofferton Junction

Extract from a Grapevine article dated August 1981 by Rev. J. T. V. Jones.

It was so easy to travel to London by train in those days. One booked straight through, took the train at Woofferton, made one change at Leominster where the direct express to London awaited one. That direct line no longer exists, even the rails and sleepers have been removed and few people standing on the far side of Leominster station would realise that the platform was a terminus for Paddington.

Woofferton was quite an active station even in my time, but in the great days of steam before the motor transport became practicable and universal it was a hive of activity, the yard filled with carts and trucks of local produce from the surrounding countryside. I have seen old photographs of the station yard being almost impenetrable with produce wagons, livestock of all kinds, fresh milk, all awaiting transport to and distribution in the large towns.

It coped with passengers, parcel and goods of all description, furniture vans, general carriages and other machines on wheels, portable engines; had provision for live stock, horse boxes and special Prize Cattle Vans. Also if you had your own carriage of the same gauge and flange it could even be attached to the train by arrangement.

One part of the station was known as Mainwaring Siding. I think this must have been named after a one-time important and influential Brimfield family named Mainwaring (pronounced Mannering) of which the last direct descendant I knew was dear Mrs. Tough who died aged 101 and so beat Miss Palfrey of Orleton by just one year. I imagine the Mainwaring family must have been amongst the railway pioneers of this stretch of track for a siding to be named after them.

Woofferton Junction 1930s
Looking towards the Station Platform. In the 1990s the building on the left is used as a plumbing and rain water stockroom for Oreton Building Supplies.

Woofferton, looking towards the Salwey Arms 1930s

Just past the black and white cottage on the left is the "Mission Room". Regular Sunday services were still held there in the 1930s and 40s. The outside appearance is still very much the same in the 1990s with the turret still remaining on the roof.

The Clarke Family, Mill Brook House 1911-1912

L to R. Edward Joseph Clarke, father, Ida Winifred Clarke, Edward Reginald Clarke, Edith Clara Clarke, mother, Bertha Marjorie Clarke, Edith Irene Clarke and Jessie the pony.

Thoughts and Deeds

A truly rural setting where in stands
An old thatched cottage, undisturbed
Then comes along the modern man
To change it all, which seems absurd.

He finds fault here and finds fault there
Then reconstructs the lot
And finally its hard to bear
When you see it go to "pot".

The sereneness and antiquity
Has never crossed the mind
And little further can he see
Than those who are so blind.

The joy and pleasure the old place gave
To those who treasured its charm
Can never again hope to save
Its uniqueness from such harm.

The love and pride that surrounded it
Can hardly be believed
And the memories that are left with it
Are precious because they are achieved.

This dear old world's gone crazy
In this so called modern age
With eyes that seem so hazy
Seeing things that are the "rage".

The world is turning inside out
As the years keep rolling by
In retrospect there is no doubt
The mistakes made, herein lie.

Let's hope there is a change of heart
To stop these stupid ways
And leave behind some treasured part
In our world, for later days.

Ida Wini Faulkner (nee Clarke)

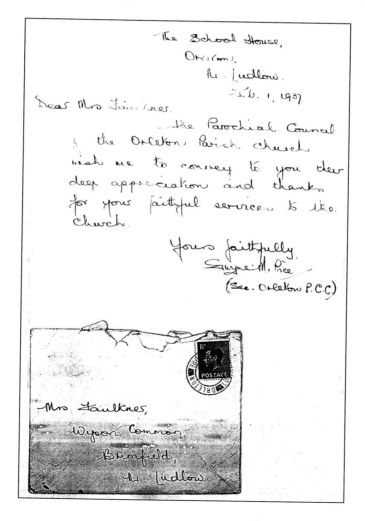

The School House,
Orleton,
Nr. Ludlow.
Feb. 1, 1937

Dear Mrs Faulkner,

The Parochial Council of the Orleton Parish Church wish me to convey to you their deep appreciation and thanks for your faithful services to the Church.

Yours faithfully,
Gwyne M. Price
(Sec. Orleton P.C.C.)

Mrs Faulkner,
Wypon Common,
Brimfield,
Nr. Ludlow.

Liverpool-Cardiff Express
Photograph taken from Tunnel Lane railway bridge 1940s

Victor Lewis often got on the train at Woofferton Junction. He spoke to the train driver and when it approached Tunnel Lane bridge he would slow down the train sufficiently to allow Victor to jump off and walk home to Inchmoor.

Recent Times

Orleton Tile Factory
Mr. Bobby Jones seen working on some of the beautiful tile creations. His factory has been established in some of the old barns alongside Orleton Manor.

Orleton Tile Factory
Local girl Hayley Cook seen perfecting an intricate design.

Orleton Evergreens 25th Anniversary, 27th May 1990
This Village Hall picture includes:- Bill Williams, Mary Williams, Nora Pegg, Jim Pegg, Vera Lloyd, Mrs. Ayres, Maude Sparey, Jessie Sparey, Eileen Morris, Mary Worthing, Kathy Godding, Adrian Sparey, Joan Edwards (Club Leader).

Recreation Ground

After purchase the original planned concept included a wooded area. A steering committee including Dr. Simon Snape, Geoff Crofts, John Cox and Margaret from The Mill put the plan into action. Mr. Ian Godding of Hi-Trees Nursery was asked to supply a variety of hardwood trees and advise on planting. On December 2nd 1989 between 60 and 70 people gathered in the proposed wooded area and set to work. In the mid 90s it is a joy to see how well established the trees are.

December 1989. Recreation Ground. Sue and Barry Rogers discuss the work in hand with Dr. Snape. Mr. Anderson is as busy as ever. Ian Godding's van in the background.

December 1989. Recreation Ground. Mrs. Kate Snape brings Ann and Alf Jenkins a hot brew.

December 1989. Recreation Ground. Hubert Wilkes and Jim Ingram take a welcome break from planting trees.

December 1989. Recreation Ground. Dr. Simon Snape, Tree planting co-ordinator looking very pleased. In the background Winifred Hinchliffe, Helen and Ian Godding.

December 1989. Excavated Pool area - Recreation Ground.

Orleton Post Office and Stores

Even in this age of the car and supermarkets, the village shop and Post Office is extremely important.

In the 1970s the proprietor Mr. Murray purchased the next door farmworker's cottage. This enabled the shop premises to be extended and offer a wider range of services. Orleton is now truly a general stores, newsagent, tobacconist, off-licence and more important still a Post Office too.

Orleton Post Office and Stores

Ruth and Andy Watson and their staff not only offer excellent service, they participate in and support village functions and encourage everyone to value the store as a communal point.

Orleton V. C. School 1990

Orleton's modern school was built in 1968. It caters for five to eleven year old children from Little Hereford, Brimfield and Orleton. The community is indeed fortunate to have excellent facilities, a pleasant environment and such a happy, welcoming atmosphere in which their children are educated.

The top picture shows a group of children in the infants class with reception teacher Mrs. Ann Harris and Headteacher Mr. Bob Parker-Morgan. The lower picture shows lunch time in the school hall. Children are being helped by Mrs. Marg. Wall and Mrs. Royle.

Orleton School, early 1990s. Mrs. Bradbury serving lunch to eagerly waiting pupils.

Mr. & Mrs. Ern Heapey outside the Bakery prior to their retirement.

1990 Co-authors of Orleton in Pictures having just printed the name of their business on their van.

Combi-Crafts 1990s

The author was trained as a cabinet maker and Handicraft teacher when he was young. In 1989 due to a deteriorating hearing loss he had to give up his Headship of Tenbury C of E Primary School. It seemed obvious to his wife Ann that he should develop his own business. As a result the two have been in partnership for seven years running Combi-Crafts which as the trade name suggests consists of sign-writing, furniture renovations and repairs, making special pieces, internal and external decorating and repairs.

Dave Lewis of Line Farm

David is an expert on working sheepdogs and has bred them for many years. If you want a good dog he is the fellow to see. It is a real country sight to see David walking briskly down Tunnel Lane with a flock of sheep running along behind him. Strange you may say to see sheep following instead of being driven and without hardly a word or command being spoken. The secret is Dave's sheepdog bringing up the rear, darting from one side of the lane to the other, nipping a straggler or creeping stealthily.

Orleton Village Hall in 1990, having just been re-decorated.

Flooding in Orleton 1990

Orleton still has its flooding problems but fortunately they do not seem as bad as they were years ago. Before the bridge was built the open ford and twisting stream caused greater flooding. In the 1930s and 40s the water often came up to the War Memorial cross roads. Jim Ingram and other lads used to borrow a large tin bath and paddle it down to the cottage by the ford to see if Nurse Powell was alright. She was frequently marooned, sitting upstairs looking out of her bedroom window for periods of a week or longer.

The author remembers in the 1960s that water came right up to the War Memorial. He and Dave Williams went by canoe to the Cottage to help remove furniture and carpets.

The top picture shows Michael Saunders standing outside the Cottage (home of Mrs. Robinson in 1996).

The bottom picture is taken from the Bridge looking towards Damson Close. You may be able to make out Chris Postons and his family in the distance on the right.

We were delighted when a new cub group was formed in Orleton in 1995. Here we see the cubs and their leaders taking part in the 1995 Remembrance Day Parade from Orleton War Memorial to the church. There the cubs' new flag was blessed by the Rev. Gareth Jones.

Inside St. George's Church, Remembrance Day 1995
Cubs brownies and guides wait for the new flag to be blessed. In the left background it is possible to discern a beautiful quilt. This was made by the Woodstock House Quilters and it represented the local churches.

The hounds meeting at The Boot Inn in the early 1990s. A country scene which may soon disappear.

The old turkey oak tree opposite Kitchen Hill. This old tree had been a landmark for many years but unfortunately became unsafe and had to be felled in the early 1990s.